'How is the mental universe of the blind, especially those blind from birth, affected by the lack of man's pre-eminent sense? [*Sight Unseen*] is a timely, absorbing and poignant exploration of this issue ... The authors' personalities shine through the dialogue: Magee is expansive, disputatious, provocative; Milligan measured, acute, reflective, to the point' *The Times*

'Magee wrote to Milligan, interrogating him about his condition, and eliciting from him some of the most striking and lucid accounts of the sightless experience that you are likely to read ... This lively exchange, between belligerent thinkers, offers an excellent introduction to issues which are so important that anybody who thinks ought to have a view about them'
Sunday Telegraph

'Philosophy in the making ... it is an enthralling book ... Here we can take the lead from the blind whose superior use of the senses they do possess gives us a clue as to how much more we might get from sight' *Spectator*

'Rather than extending our sensory horizons, we are reminded of the seamless, but ineluctable net of language, and learn more of its extraordinary nature. And that itself is fascinating'
Times Higher Educational Supplement

'Unusual, moving ... Magee [is] a beautifully lucid writer'
Times Literary Supplement

'Superb ... a lively and acute philosophical dialogue pitched at a high level of intellectual seriousness, written in the readable style of a letter to a pal, and kindled by the full range of human reflexes' *Independent*

Bryan Magee has been a Member of Parliament, a critic of music and theatre, and a professional broadcaster. He has various honorary academic appointments, including Visiting Professor at King's College, University of London; Fellow of Queen Mary College, London; and Fellow of Keble College, Oxford. His books include *The Philosophy of Schopenhauer*, *The Great Philosophers*, *Aspects of Wagner* and *Confessions of a Philosopher*.

The late Martin Milligan was Head of Department in Philosophy at the University of Leeds until shortly before his death; he had been there since 1959. He was a well-known blind activist, campaigning for the equal treatment, and integration into sighted society, of blind people.

Sight Unseen

Letters between
BRYAN MAGEE
AND
MARTIN MILLIGAN

PHŒNIX

A PHOENIX PAPERBACK

First published in Great Britain
by Oxford University Press in 1995
as *On Blindness*
Published in the United States by
Oxford University Press Inc., New York
This paperback edition published in 1998 by Phoenix
a division of Orion Books Ltd,
Orion House, 5 Upper St Martin's Lane,
London WC2H 9EA

A CIP catalogue record for this book
is available from the British Library.

ISBN: 0 75380 503 0

Typeset at The Spartan Press Ltd,
Lymington, Hants
Printed and bound in Great Britain by
The Guernsey Press Co. Ltd,
Guernsey, Channel Islands

To

ROBIN DAY

who suggested the title

CONTENTS

Introduction

BRYAN MAGEE

To a sighted person few thoughts are as horrific as that of having one's eyeballs removed, but I have known two people to whom it has happened, in babyhood. Both had a disease which was, in effect, a cancer of the eyes; and at that time (not now) the only way known of ensuring that the cancer did not spread to the brain was to remove the eyes. Both men, it so happened, became distinguished academics – Rupert Cross at Oxford, where he was Professor of English Law, and Martin Milligan at Leeds, where he was head of the philosophy department and Dean of the Faculty of Arts.

Martin had a dramatic, almost melodramatic, life. He was born in Scotland in 1923 into a working-class family, and spent his childhood in one of Britain's most notorious slum areas, the Gorbals of Glasgow. But he had the good fortune to be educated together with sighted children, and not segregated, because by sheer chance he was caught up in an experiment conducted by an enlightened local authority. In spite of the twin handicaps of social deprivation and blindness he was so successful academically that he entered the University of Edinburgh at the age of sixteen and graduated at nineteen. From there he gained a scholarship to Balliol College, Oxford, where he was awarded first-class honours in Philosophy, Politics and Economics and launched into post-graduate work on Hegel's philosophy of history. His aim then was to become a university teacher of philosophy. But for a number of years the world, having been so kind to him up to that point, brutally frustrated his aspirations.

At bottom this was largely because he had become, before the phrase was coined, an angry young man. He was enraged by the way blind people in those days were patronized and discriminated against. Above all he was incensed by the way they were normally segregated and thus prevented from sharing in the common life of their own society. He knew he had been exceptionally lucky in these respects, and he set himself to extend to blind people in general the benefits that he himself had enjoyed. The last thing he wanted was to be the sort of smiling, co-operative blind person who goes along with whatever happens and whom everybody likes. Instead he became a fierce, bile-in-the-mouth campaigner against both the *status quo* and other peoples' complacent acceptance of it, and remained so for the rest of his life.

For blind people he had two goals above all. First, that they should achieve autonomy and self-respect both as individuals and as groups, running their own lives and organizations on equal terms with the sighted as far as is humanly possible, not treated as incapables who have to have everything done for them. Second, that they should be fully accepted members of society at the same time, living, working, playing, being educated and so on, alongside and in amongst the sighted, with every door open to them. He was practical in his approach to these aims and helped to devise enabling techniques of all sorts (for instance advanced braille codes), set up new organizations, change existing ones, get the law altered, and so on and so forth. In Britain the campaign to integrate visually handicapped children into mainstream education owes more to him than to any other individual. When he was in his prime there can have been few people anywhere who achieved as much for the blind as he did.

But his zeal for revolutionary change went beyond the affairs of the blind. During his student days he joined the Communist Party, of which he remained a member until the last decade of his life. It was this party affiliation on top of everything else that for a long time turned so much of the world against him. Confronted by a strident, highly intelligent, articulate and aggressive blind Communist, people were scared of having him as a colleague. They thought it was bound to mean trouble, especially as they knew they would feel inhibited about fighting him on account of his blindness. So he was unable to get an academic job. An additional and important reason for this was that as a Marxist he was wedded to a thought-system which most professional philosophers regarded as not merely out-moded but fundamentally erroneous.

So Martin was forced to look for work outside academe. But he found it difficult to get that too. Again, it was probably his communism more than his blindness that created the obstacle: employers saw him as a potential source of trouble, and one they would be unable to get tough about because of his blindness. For twelve years Martin earned his living in work, often part-time, that was absurdly below the level of his abilities, for instance as a shorthand-typist. Often he had no work at all, and had to live off his parents. These were black and bitter years for him, all the more so because there was no reason to believe at the time that his luck was ever going to change. But he never stopped striving for what he believed he could do, and in 1959, at the age of thirty-six, his persistence was rewarded. He was appointed to a full-time job in the philosophy depart-ment at the University of Leeds.

Neither adversity nor his own crusading spirit made Martin narrow. There was always room in his life for things that had nothing to do with any of the activities I have mentioned. For instance, he was a talented pianist, good enough to broadcast on BBC radio a number of times as an accompanist in song recitals. The singer on those occasions was Jeanette Goddard, his first wife, also blind. She seemed set for success, having not only broadcast but given a well-reviewed solo recital at the Wigmore Hall; but she gave up her singing career on having a baby. This was Martin's only child, likewise christened Martin. The son of two blind parents, Martin the younger was, though visually handicapped, not blind.

This is not the place to launch into an extended biography of the older Martin, though one day his life should be recounted with the amplitude it deserves. It combines a diversity of interesting stories – not only the blindness story but also the Gorbals-to-Oxford story, and the communism and anti-communism stories; and others too: for example he was attractive to women, and there are stories to be told about that, including those of his three marriages. But as far as introducing the present volume is concerned, having followed his life to the point where he became a professional philosopher we must turn now to the correspondence in this book and the story of how it began.

From the seventeenth century to the twentieth many philosophers considered the most important question to be 'What can I know?' Some, such as Berkeley, and many if not most twentieth-century philosophers, believed that what I can know is what there is. But I have never seen good reason for believing this. From my own reflections, and also from studying Locke, Hume and Kant, I am persuaded that the world we know is phenomenon and not at all the same as reality as it is regardless of experience. However, if the forms taken by the deliverances of consciousness are inherently subject-dependent, the question arises how, if at all, we can know what the relationship is between the deliverances of consciousness and whatever reality there may be that is not subject-dependent. Many have held that we never can: that we live in an epistemological cage from which there is no escape. But a long time ago now I came to think there may be a rational way in which we can get a worthwhile indication of what sort of relationship our relationship to the unknowable is.

The main line of thought was this. We have these major senses of sight, hearing and touch which provide us with most of the raw materials from which we construct our conception of the empirical world. Anything that these or our other senses, and our nervous systems, and our brains, are able to mediate is usable material for us. But anything that falls outside that – anything that exists that we cannot apprehend or conceptualize or feel – has no being *for us*, real though it is. Now the fact that we have the particular physical apparatus that we do have is a contingent fact, not a necessary one. We do not know what sort of senses and mental abilities we might have had yet do not have: but we do know that if we had even only one or two of them, and they were of the same scale of distinctiveness and significance as seeing and hearing, our conception of reality would be hugely different from what it is. If we had such senses in addition to our existing ones our conception of the world would contain everything it contains now plus whole dimensions which *ex hypothesi* would make as much difference to us as seeing and hearing do but which we cannot conceptualize in specific terms. However, we do have, already, within the range of human experience as it is now, the means of acquiring an understanding of what *sort* of difference that difference is. For there are some human beings who have never had sight, and others who have never had hearing (and some, like Helen Keller, who were without either). If we can get an understanding of the difference this makes to the conception of reality they have as compared with the rest of us, that surely might give us an indication of what sort of difference the limitations that all of us share make to all of us? Just as the visual world is there, even though blind people cannot see it, and was there before sighted creatures evolved, and would still be there if sighted creatures had never come into existence, so, presumably, whole dimensions of reality, into which a sensory apparatus different from any that any of us possess would plug us, may well be there all the time without our knowing. If that is so then in some ways the relationship of all of us, all human beings, to those unapprehended dimensions of reality may be similar to the relationship of the congenitally blind to the visual world.

I was thinking along these lines when I went to All Souls College, Oxford, as a Visiting Fellow in 1973. There I met Rupert Cross, who had been without eyes since babyhood; and I put these thoughts to him. Although he was an academic lawyer he had always taken a lively interest in philosophy and he understood how my questions, as well as being independently interesting, related to issues fundamental to Western philosophy. He became involved, and we had long discussions which remain to this day among the most interesting I have ever taken part in. They led me to suggest that we write a book together, and he agreed. We were both currently working on other books, so the agreement was that we would start to collaborate after we had finished with these. Alas, the collaboration never began: he died before finishing the book he was working on.

It did not occur to me immediately to pursue the project with someone else: I mourned for Rupert, I did not know of anyone who was suitable, and in any case I was busy with other things. But the fundamental question of whether there was some valuable insight to be gained in this way nagged at the back of my mind for many years. Eventually I decided to make another attempt to pursue it.

I made enquiries as to whether there was such a thing in England as a professional philosopher who had been blind from birth, and heard of the existence of Martin Milligan in Leeds. We had long, promising discussions on the telephone before we met. Then, because of the difficulties involved in meeting, we decided to pursue the discussion in the form of a correspondence. In order that no confusion should be caused in either of our minds by unspoken assumptions that turned out not to be shared, it was agreed that I should launch the correspondence with a letter that started the whole subject off from scratch. And so the letters in this volume came to be written.

Almost immediately, the correspondence hared off in a direction that I had not foreseen. But that meant that almost from the beginning I found myself learning unexpected things. After Martin's death, which will be explained later, I found myself reflecting that other readers might do the same. The following letters are published in that hope.

Letter 1

FROM **BRYAN MAGEE**

TO **MARTIN MILLIGAN**

Dear Martin,

As a professional philosopher who have, or so I have been told, been blind all your life, you are in a position to make a special contribution to the discussion of fundamental problems in philosophy, it seems to me.

Most of the greatest philosophers of the last three hundred years have held that all our knowledge about the world, about what actually exists, must ultimately derive from experience. It is not only philosophers in the empiricist tradition who have held this view. The opening sentence of the Introduction to Kant's *Critique of Pure Reason* runs: 'There can be no doubt that all our knowledge begins with experience'. Schopenhauer was of the same opinion, as have been many great philosophers whom no one would call empiricists. Although not all philosophers during this period have been of one mind, it would certainly be true to say that this opinion has been held by most of those whom you and most other people professionally involved in philosophy are accustomed to thinking of as 'great' philosophers.

The raw material of our experience comes to us through our sensory and nervous systems. And in the popular mind, at least, the most important of our senses is sight. I am not myself sure that this assumption is correct. I suspect that the hardest sense to live without would be that of feeling, touch; but even if that is true I would still have to acknowledge that sight comes second in importance among our five senses. In either case you are without one of the primary sources of perception and experience on which human beings in general rely. So the question arises: What difference does this make to your knowledge? What difference does it make to the *forms* your knowledge takes? What difference does it make to the formation of your concepts? What difference does it make to your conception of the world?

Let me take, as an example, our ordinary conception of what it is to know a person. If I think of someone I know, an image of that person's visual appearance at once leaps into my mind. I have discussed this with other sighted people, and find that this seems to be the common experience. And on further discussion we agree that it is difficult for us to imagine what it is like to know a person without any conception at all of his or her visual appearance. We have considered instances of people who talk to one another frequently and at length on the telephone over a period of years without having met, and of people who are pen friends for many years without meeting, but in all such cases we find ourselves uncomfortable about saying that these people 'really know' one another. Until they have *seen* one another we feel like withholding the qualification 'really know'. What we tend to find, on excavating our experience, is that in the case of human beings a visual image is the nub to which all other associations need to be attached before we have the sense of relating directly to an entity (the person) and not just to one or some of the manifestations of that entity (a voice; letters).

Now obviously none of this applies to you. You have married, and brought up a child. You have had a full and successful academic career, becoming head of your department at a famous university, with everything implied by this whole process in terms of relationships with colleagues and students. You have been a political activist for many years. You have also been active in national organizations for the blind. One way and another you seem to have lived a rich and many-sided life; perpetually involved with other people in a range of human relationships that stretches from the most private and intimate to the most public and impersonal. Yet you do not know what anyone looks like. In fact, if it is true that all our empirical concepts must derive ultimately from experience, you can have no empirically based conception of what a visual appearance is, and therefore cannot have any such conception of what it means for anyone or anything to have a visual appearance at all, and therefore cannot know what it is for anyone to look like anything. This forces me to the conclusion that your concept of 'knowing a person' must be importantly different from mine. More than that, it suggests that your concept of a person is different from mine. What, in either case, does the difference consist in? And what practical difference do these differences make? Can they be articulated in language? Is it possible for me to understand fully what they are? Would it be possible for me to know someone in the same way as you do without myself being blind?

These questions are interesting in themselves. But I have an ulterior motive in raising them with you. It is that they go to the heart of not one but several of the issues that lie at the foundations of philosophy. How do we acquire our knowledge and understanding of the world, including our knowledge of one another? What is the relationship between knowledge and experience? Is what we can understand limited by what we can experience? Is what can be communicated in language limited by the experience of the language-users? Might there have been a large, perhaps indefinitely large, number of other senses that we humans could have had but happen not to have, each one of which would make as much difference to our conception of the world as sight or the lack of it does to you and me? If there is not, why is there not? Surely I can imagine that our bodies might have been equipped to register and interpret radio and television waves, radar, and all sorts of other rays and waves, in much the same way as we happen to be equipped to register and interpret light rays and sound waves? And if they had been, would not the human conception of the world have been radically different throughout pre-history and history from what it has been? The same point can be put the other way round. Some people are born blind, and it would have been possible for everyone to be born blind. If that had happened, the conception of the world we humans as a whole would possess, and the civilization we would have created, would surely be almost unimaginably different from what they actually are.

For reasons implicit in all this it seems to me that if, in dialogue with each other, we can find a way of coming to grips with these questions, the fact that I am sighted and you are blind may enable us to reach worthwhile conclusions about important issues. Would you be willing to give it a try, by launching into a correspondence with me and seeing what happens? It will involve starting, at least, by digging into this discrepancy between us and trying to understand what difference it makes. It will involve digging also into the intelligibility to each of us of the difference – and that will open up the question of the communicability of experience, indeed of whole modes of experience, to a person who has never had anything that corresponds to them.

Because the basic themes of our discussion will include the limits of intelligibility and the limits of language I am aware from the outset that we are up against my limitations as well as yours. But most human beings are in my situation, not in yours; so I suggest that you launch our discussion by putting forward preliminary answers to two questions. (I say 'preliminary' because you will obviously be free to add or qualify as much as you like as we go along.) First, what in actual experience are the chief ways in which you are made aware of the fact that you lack a sense that others have? Second, what conception do you have of the nature of this missing sense?

Yours ever,
Bryan

Letter 2

FROM MARTIN MILLIGAN
TO BRYAN MAGEE

Dear Bryan,

Thank you very much for your letter and for inviting me to join you in exploring some questions of philosophic interest by way of an extended exchange of letters about being blind. The prospect of engaging in such an exchange with you is a very agreeable one. I must confess, though, that I'm a little afraid of turning out a bit of a disappointment to you.

It is true that I have been blind for almost the whole of my life. But I was not actually born blind. For the first eighteen months of my life I could, apparently, see perfectly well; but it then became clear that, due (as is now thought) to a mutation in my genetic make-up, I had retinoblastoma as it has come to be called, i.e. cancer of the retinas, for which the only known treatment at that time was removal of the eyes to prevent the tumour from speading into the brain. My eyes were therefore promptly removed, and I have not seen since.

More to the point, perhaps: although I am assured that I have seen, I have no memory of doing so, and therefore I cannot directly contrast for myself my present sensory experience with what it was when I could see.

This inability does not arise simply, as might be thought, from my having lacked for a long time any .visual experience which could, as it is put, 'awaken' the memory of seeing. There are blind adults who have never seen since the age of six or seven, say, who do not need any such 'awakening' experience, but say that they remember what it was like to see, and that they have continued to have dreams full of visual imagery for twenty, thirty or more years after their loss of sight. I have never heard, however, of anyone who lost their sight before the age of two who in later life dreamt visually, or remembered what it was like to see. In any case, I don't. Very likely the stage in one's life to which one's memory can reach back varies a good deal from individual to individual. Certainly individuals vary greatly in what they *claim* to be able to remember. But I doubt if anyone has memories of every stage of development through which they have passed since conception. In any case, I have not uncovered in myself any memory relating to a period earlier than my fourth year of life, which is long after my complete loss of sight. For the purposes of our discussion it is just as if I had been born blind, and I shall count myself with the blind-from-birth – for no matter how many visual experiences I had had, and no matter when I had lost my sight, if I *have* lost it *and* have no memory of having had it the question which you put to me at the end of your letter as to how I am made aware that I lack a sense that others have still has force for me in a way that it would not for people now blind who remember seeing. Such people could answer it by saying that one of the chief ways in which they are made aware of their lack is that they remember past experience which had in it an important constituent which their present experience is without. I cannot give that answer.

So I agree that my condition does give rise to at least one question of philosophic interest – namely, in effect, 'How do I know that I am blind?'; or, if you prefer, 'Why do I think it reasonable to believe that I am blind?' I also agree that all the other questions which you set out in your letter are extremely interesting questions to whose discussion someone in my condition might well be expected to contribute something. But although I have been professionally concerned with philosophy for a considerable part of my life, and have occasionally reflected a little about some of these questions, the fact is that I have never got far with such reflections until now. Perhaps this has been due chiefly to the fact that both my teaching duties and the lie of my own main interests have caused me to be preoccupied with issues in moral and political philosophy, and in the philosophy of history and of the social sciences, which are pretty remote from those issues to which my being blind could be immediately relevant. Even in my younger days, when I had an active interest in the theory of knowledge and related areas of philosophy, I still didn't get much out of my blindness. Part of my reason for fearing that I may be a disappointment to you is that I am sure that I was a disappointment then to at least one philosopher who hoped that I as a blind person might be able to say something of interest about philosophic matters. As an undergraduate at Oxford during the Second World War I had the good fortune for a while to have as a tutor Professor H. H. Price, who, you will know, had a strong interest in philosophic issues connected with perception. I remember his summing up of the experience of teaching me for a term by saying that I was 'too clever'. This was clearly understood by me and by my college to be no compliment but gentle disparagement. What he meant was that I could get up the stuff in the books all right, and argue about it, but that I didn't bring my own experience as a blind person to bear on problems where it would have been relevant. I admitted to myself the validity of this challenge, and indeed of other challenges that occasionally came my way, to think about the nature and significance of my own experience as a blind person. Nevertheless I never responded seriously to these challenges.

You have now renewed this sort of challenge in a particularly attractive way, so that I do now want to respond. But I can't help feeling that if I'd got much of interest to say about blindness, I'd have started saying it before now. I take comfort from the reply you made to me in our preliminary conversation about this project – that it didn't matter if I felt at first that I hadn't anything interesting to say about my blindness because *you* had interesting questions to *ask* about it. I think that may be quite right. You *do* pose interesting questions, and already I am beginning to feel the hope stir that something might emerge from a dialogue between the two of us which I would not have been able to get out of myself.

Anyway, let's have a go. I enter on this enquiry with some inclinations about how to begin to reply to some of your questions, but without clear or firmly-fixed ideas about the conclusions I either expect or want us to reach. I am looking forward to finding out as we go along not only what you think, but also what I myself think, about a number of questions in the field you have indicated.

Much as I am tempted to take up immediately some of the other questions you raise in your letter, I will confine myself for the moment to the two with which, at the end of your letter, you ask me to begin. You ask, first: 'What in actual experience are the chief ways in which you are made aware that you lack a sense that others have?'

What I am immediately inclined to say is that my experience furnishes me daily with a great deal of evidence that others can *do* things which I can't. To take only two very obvious instances out of thousands: many people, apparently without any great effort, can walk down an unfamiliar, noisy street unaided by a stick or a dog, or any other external equipment, and without asking anyone can find, let us say, a travel agent's office. Others, again, can drive a bus for hours on end through busy traffic without bumping into anything or knocking anyone down. I couldn't do these things; and this difference in capacity might reasonably be thought to suggest that others have something I haven't got.

Now that sort of answer is all right as far as it goes, and indeed I think it is more fundamental than another answer that might spring to mind, which is that, even without doing anything, others often appear to *know* things that I don't. They confidently answer questions such as 'Is the light on in this room?' or 'How is he looking?' to which I don't know the answers, and about whose very meaning, in some cases, I am not wholly clear.

I say that the answer about doing is more fundamental than the answer about knowing because I don't think that I would initially be too ready to allow that people who can apparently make sense of and answer questions which I can't should straightway be credited with having knowledge that I don't have. I might think that those people who talk about light and colour were suffering from some sort of weird delusion. But if I could perceive that they were able to do a very large number of things which I can't do, and if they associated this with their claim to have extra knowledge, I would feel that I would have to be more respectful towards that claim. You may remember that in H. G. Wells's story *The Country of the Blind* it is the failure of the lone sighted man to *do* things which they can't do; and his failure even to do all the things which, in their society geared to the needs and abilities of blind people, they *can* do; which persuades the blind people that the strange protuberances which they have found in the front of his face are a defect and a source of derangement, rather than an asset and a source of knowledge, as he claims.

The answer that others can do things which I can't is, however, too broad, because it doesn't by itself go far enough. Many others can converse in Urdu or play the violin, and I can do neither of these things; but I don't put *those* differences between me and others down to their having a *sense*, a source of knowledge based on a specific feature of the body, which I lack. Why do I put *some* though not all of the differences between my abilities and the abilities of many others down to the possession by them of an extra sense? To that question the obvious answer might seem to be that when I ask people how they manage to find a particular shop in a noisy unfamiliar street, or drive a vehicle without constantly crashing into things, they answer that they can *see* where the shop or the other vehicles and obstacles are; and that they associate this claim, when pressed, with the assertion that, as they put it, their eyes are open and working all right and that there is enough light.

But *you* are asking of course how this answer makes any sense to me, since I can't see now and can't remember seeing. You rightly point out that if one accepts what seems to be a fairly straightforward interpretation of the old and influential philosophic belief that there can be nothing in the mind which has not first been in the senses – or, indeed, of weaker or more sophisticated versions of that belief – then it would seem that one would have to conclude that a person blind from birth, or a person like myself in a similar position, simply cannot attach any sense to visual terms. Yet I certainly do attach some sense to such terms. It does make sense to me for people to say that they can see – more than it would if they were to claim that they can, say, 'scridge', for that last claim would be quite unintelligible to me. I would not know in this last case what sort of thing was being claimed.

Probably when I was first told by my mother that she could

see something, that was as unintelligible as would be the claim that someone can scridge. But presumably in my early childhood she and others were constantly saying things of all kinds that I did not understand. Nor did they always, or even perhaps often, offer definitions of the words I did not understand. But if they went on using unintelligible words a lot, as people certainly did in the case of the words 'see', 'light' and 'dark', I suppose I began to get some idea of when and why such words were used, and how they were usually placed in relation to one another and to other words.

I must make it clear that I don't remember a time when I was totally baffled by such words as 'see', 'light' and 'dark'. But no doubt there was such a time, when these were among the many words whose use I did not yet 'get'. I suppose I must have begun to catch on when my parents and others claimed to see things without touching or listening which I could find out by touching or listening *only*. If they said with confidence that they could see that my toy was under the table, and I then crawled under the table and found it there, I would be inclined, I suppose, to credit them with knowledge of the same thing as I knew when I touched the toy, but gained in a way not open to me. And if on occasion they would say that they couldn't see where my toy was, because it was too dark, I would gather that this way of knowing, open to them but not to me, was not even open to them under all conditions; and that 'darkness' was the term for a condition in which they could not exercise their extra way of knowing. I would therefore pick up the idea that 'seeing' was the term for a way of coming by information of a kind that could also be obtained, but often less quickly, by touching or listening, and that, like touching or hearing, it was a way of getting to know things dependent partly on parts of the body functioning well, and partly on external conditions. In other

12

words, as I eventually learned to say, sight was a 'sense'. To understand this about the word 'see' is to understand more than I understand about the word 'scridge', and it is to understand something very important, something which is quite enough to make meaningful for me the proposition that I am blind.

To put this point in a less 'psychological' and perhaps more 'philosophical' way, there really is no difficulty in principle, any more than there is in practice, in a person with some senses, who also has some powers of making and receiving communications, and powers of reasoning, recognising that others may have more or fewer senses than he or she has. And it seems clear that, provided they share a common language, a person with fewer senses than others might *know* many things – involving being conscious of having good reasons for believing them, and of an absence of good reasons for doubting them – which have not first been in that person's own senses, though they would have to have been first in *somebody's* senses.

But perhaps you might object that the reference to a 'common language' begs the whole question again. Do blind and sighted people share a common language, you may ask, when in fact sighted people are constantly using words which cannot at least have the *same* meaning for blind people as they have for the sighted? Well, I have already argued that at least part, and I would say a very major part, of the meaning of such words as 'see', 'light' and 'dark' is the same for blind as for sighted people. For both blind and sighted 'see' means, at least, having a kind of awareness of things dependent on the functioning of the eyes; and 'light' and 'dark' mean respectively the presence and absence of a condition permitting this kind of awareness.

Perhaps it's just worth dwelling for a moment on the word 'darkness', to emphasise that for blind-from-birth people and people like me this word doesn't have any direct experiential significance. We don't live, as is sometimes supposed, in a 'world of darkness', because, not knowing directly from our own experience anything about light, we don't have any direct experience of darkness. Nevertheless, we can understand what I think can be called the primary meaning of 'darkness' as being 'a state of affairs where there is little or no light'; and, as I have already said, 'light' can be understood by blind people as 'that which makes things visible'; and 'visible' as 'object of a kind of awareness specifically associated with the use of eyes'. There are (abbreviated versions of) dictionary meanings of these words, and blind-from-birth people can grasp them and use the words in accordance with them just as well as sighted people. I can go further and say that for blind people, because of the ways in which such words are so frequently used by sighted people in common talk, stories, and abstract argument, a word such as 'darkness' has all the secondary meanings or associations which it has for sighted people – associations with *difficulty* in perception, with the unknown and the incomprehensible, with threat and danger, and also sometimes with warmth, privacy and safety against intrusive perceptions by others. This body of central meaning and associated suggestion can be shared between sighted and blind people because it is not dependent on all users of the words having visual experience. Since 'sight' is a species of the genus 'perception' of which blind people do have some experience, they know the *sort* of thing sighted people are talking about, and can come to accept, even themselves to talk sensibly about, a species of the genus with which they are not personally acquainted.

I think you will grant all this; and in granting it you will be granting that blind people do really have a conception of sight, that it is as I have indicated above, and that I have therefore already answered the second of the two questions at the end of your letter: 'What conception do you have of the nature of this missing sense?' It is, I would say – to go just a little further for the time being – a sense more like hearing than the other senses, since through it one can obtain information about things with which the body is not in immediate contact. It is also like hearing in that, just as blind people at least can hear objects, and thus make something of their surroundings, as well as hear sounds (a matter I should perhaps say a word more about some time), so we can understand that sighted people, through sight, can get not just visual data but an awareness of objects and surroundings, and one which is evidently both more comprehensive and more detailed than one can get through the ears alone.

I hope that you will agree that the conception of sight held by a blind-from-birth person or his like is at least partly the same as any sighted person's conception of sight. But I can imagine you saying 'Yes, partly, but by no means *wholly* the same'. For I imagine that you might want to argue that for people who have seen, visual terms must have a meaning that they cannot have for people who have not seen.

I think there are contemporary philosophers – for instance, at least some followers of Wittgenstein – who would dispute that, and say that since blind people can use visual terms correctly and purposefully and *receive*, through the use by others of such terms, any propositional knowledge possessed by sighted people, they should not be said just to know *part* of the meaning of visual terms, but to know their meaning completely, and indeed to be *able* to know everything that sighted people can know. Blind people can use visual words just as well as sighted people, they might say, the only difference between the two groups being that blind people often do not in fact have the knowledge that sighted people have, although they are perfectly capable of acquiring it.

It seems to me that there is a great deal of truth in this view. Nevertheless I am inclined to agree with you – and, I think, with the overwhelming majority of ordinary sighted and blind people – in thinking that there is something which blind-from-birth people don't know which is known to people who can see or remember seeing, and that there is therefore a part of the meaning of visual terms to which blind-from-birth people and blind people like me have no access. That is what I was referring to earlier when I used the rather pompous phrase 'experiential significance'. I can bring out what I mean by recalling a story which was in the newspapers some time ago about a woman who had been blind since infancy, but who, late in life, got some sight for the first time. I agree that this woman would certainly say (surely persuasively) that she had come to know something after she got her sight which she had never known previously. But really it is not easy, is it, to say precisely what she has come to know; because if she were to say simply that she has come to know what it is to see, I have argued that she already knew a good deal about that when she was blind and knew she was blind. If she were to say, as she very well might, that she has come to know what it is *like* to see – well, again, I think we must say that she knew when she was blind that seeing was, up to a point, like touching or hearing, etc.; and it seems very probable that after gaining her sight she won't be able to say anything more about what seeing is like than she could before she could see.

Maybe you will reply that this new knowledge she has is experiential knowledge, not propositional knowledge, and that the part of the meaning of visual terms which blind-from-birth people can't share is their reference to inner experience. I would probably then want to ask how sighted people can know that they have the same inner experiences of seeing as one another – and why, if they *can* know this, blind people can't know something about this inner experience too. But it's time for me to stop guessing about what you might say, and to leave you to speak for yourself. Perhaps you would say what you think of my contentions so far, and also how you would go on from where I've got stuck. Do you agree that blind people can understand the meaning of visual terms to a major extent, but not wholly; and if so, what would you say about the part of their meaning that blind people can't share?

Yours ever,
Martin

Letter 3

FROM BRYAN MAGEE
TO MARTIN MILLIGAN

Dear Martin,

Your letter convinces me that we can make progress, because
there are things in it that surprise me and yet whose validity I
find myself acknowledging. There are also things that I want to
take issue with – or at least that I am not prepared to go along
with, as yet – and if in any of those cases I come to realize that I
am mistaken, that too will be progress, at least for me.

The first thing in your letter that pulled me up short was your
reformulation of my first question to you as: 'How do I know
that I am blind?' or 'Why do I think it reasonable to believe that I
am blind?' To a sighted person this is startling. It seems that *of
course* blind people must know they are blind. How can they
possibly not know they are blind? An illustration of this is that
when I told a friend – who is also, incidentally, a retired
Professor of Philosophy – that I had embarked on this correspondence with you, his first response was to say: 'But why
does he need to correspond with you? Why doesn't he just write
a book about what it's like being blind? After all, it's him who's
blind.' And only then, as an afterthought, he added: 'But I
suppose if he's never been able to see he doesn't fully understand the difference it makes.'

What you say goes to the heart of some of the problems we

shall be discussing. Among other things it drives home the fact that blind-from-birth people have no direct experiential awareness of lacking anything. The sighted think of them as living in permanent blackness, and of this as being a terrifying affliction. But you tell me – and as soon as you say it I realize it must be true – that the blind-from-birth do not inhabit a world of darkness at all. The concept 'darkness' has no experiential content for them, just as the concepts 'light' and 'sight' have no experiential content, and they have no way of understanding experientially what it means to say of someone that he lives in darkness. So they no more feel a sense of deprivation on that score than I do because I lack an indefinite number of possible senses that I might have had but do not have, and cannot imagine.

For all of us the sensory equipment that we have or lack is a contingent matter, and there are all sorts of senses that we might have had but do not have. Many living creatures are equipped with senses that all humans lack – some bats have a sort of radar – but it never occurs to us to think of ourselves as handicapped because we lack them. We do not suffer a sense of deprivation because our bodies are not equipped to hear any sound waves above or below a certain narrow band of frequencies, or register any light waves above or below a narrow band of frequencies, or because they do not have the power to transmit and receive television or radio signals – any more than we feel that our freedom is limited by the fact that we are unable to be in two places at once. We do not even feel deprived by the fact that the senses we do have work a lot less well than they might. Hosts of familiar animals have a far more powerful and discriminating sense of smell than humans do, and I am told that there are moths that can smell a possible mate four miles away, but we humans do not feel ourselves to be deprived because of this. Hawks, kestrels and lynxes clearly see and respond to details that are invisible to the sighted human, but that does not cause sighted humans to feel visually handicapped. In practice we take completely and utterly for granted the equipment that is ours – and then take reality to be whatever we apprehend by means of that equipment.

A great many living creatures have no power of sight at all, and it would have been possible for all humans to have no such power. If that had been the case, what we now call 'sight' would have been one of that indefinite number of additional senses which we know to be possible in principle but are unable to imagine. The very concept 'sight' would not then be able to exist, because no basis for it would ever have been in anyone's experience. The word would be, as you would say, like 'scridge', to all of us. As a species we would have no sense whatever of being handicapped in that regard, no sense of lacking anything. This point is superbly made in H. G. Wells's story *The Country of the Blind*, to which your letter directed me and which I was greatly impressed by. It is possible for the sightless to be looked on as handicapped, or to feel themselves to be handicapped, only and solely because there are people who can see. Your argument that the blind can know quite a lot about what it is to see rests on their being able to understand things sighted people say that involve visual experience. But, as you concede, that experience needs first to have been in somebody or something's senses for this to be possible. If everybody and everything shared that particular limitation none of us would have any way of knowing that we had it.

And this, of course, raises a fundamental fact about human beings as such. What we think of as fully equipped human beings are human beings who share the same sensory limitations. This being the case we do not normally think of them as limitations. However, if we were all at the same time to acquire an additional and major sense on a par in significance with feeling and hearing we would suddenly acquire with it a fundamentally altered conception of reality – just as we would if we had all been blind from birth and then suddenly began to see. It would be for us as if reality had been transfigured, though of course the whole new dimension of which we became aware would be explained in terms of our new sense, and therefore in terms of us and our apparatus, not in terms of reality as having changed.

Bertrand Russell makes this last point penetratingly with reference to light in *The Problems of Philosophy* (pp. 28–9). It is a passage worth quoting in full:

It is sometimes said that 'light *is* a form of wave motion', but this is misleading, for the light which we immediately see, which we know directly by means of our senses, is *not* a form of wave-motion, but something quite different – something which we all know if we are not blind, though we cannot describe it so as to convey our knowledge to a man who is blind. A wave-motion, on the contrary, could quite well be described to a blind man, since he can acquire a knowledge of space by the sense of touch; and he can experience a wave-motion by a sea voyage almost as well as we can. But this, which a blind man can understand, is not what we mean by *light*: we mean by *light* just that which a blind man can never understand, and which we can never describe to him.

Now this something, which all of us who are not blind know, is not, according to science, really to be found in the outer world: it is something caused by the action of certain waves upon the eyes and nerves and brain of the person who sees the light. When it is said that light *is* waves, what is really meant is that waves are the physical cause of our sensations of light. But light itself, the thing which seeing people experience and blind people do not, is not supposed by science to form any part of the world that is independent of us and our senses. And very similar remarks would apply to other kinds of sensations.

When I first read this passage it gave me a shock. I was disturbed to have it brought home to me fully for the first time that light is not a characteristic of the world independent of experience, does not exist out there 'in reality' but is only, so to speak, 'in my head'. I even found it frightening, as if I were moving through an alien, lightless world with an unreliable and fragile lamp perched precariously in my forehead – as if, so to speak, I were a vulnerable oasis in a desert of blindness. The passage thrust piercingly into my awareness something that is difficult to grasp, and something I suspect most people never do grasp, namely that we cannot necessarily attribute the characteristics of our experience to reality as it exists independently of us and our perceiving apparatus. It is not just that we have no warrant for supposing reality to be as it is presented to us by that apparatus: we actually know that in many respects, as in this case of light, it cannot be. Of course, that is the only way we can *envisage* reality, because all our conceptions of the empirical world, insofar as they have genuine content, can derive only from deliverances to somebody's consciousness from his sensory and mental apparatus. Anything no one's consciousness is able to register is incomprehensible to all of us. Therefore, inevitably, we identify reality with our human experience of it. No alternative to that is available to us. That is the reason for what Schopenhauer calls 'the inborn realism that arises from the original disposition of the intellect'. But it would have been, even if it were possible, a coincidence of astounding proportions if existent reality, which after all is itself contingent, were to have corresponded to the apparatus for monitoring it that we humans happened to have developed.

Someone might want to protest: 'Oh, no, it wouldn't. That apparatus evolved over millions of years precisely for the task of coping with our environment. We should therefore expect a match between the equipment and the environment, and if there were no such match we would not be able to survive.' But to that at least part of the answer is that all living entities whatsoever, past as well as present, have emerged in the same process of evolution, and contain among themselves a distribution of almost incredibly widely differing sets of equipment for coping with life on the same little planet; and in this overall distribution there is a vast number of items that we humans do not share. So there is a vast number of aspects of reality that are apprehended by other creatures but not by us. This and other considerations already touched on render it certain that there can be no 'match' in the sense in which people usually understand it between what we apprehend and reality as it is, that our total environment does not 'correspond' to our conception of it, and could not. Indeed, there is a deep mystery about what 'correspond' could even so much as mean in this context. It is difficult to see in what sense existent material objects could 'correspond to' or 'be like' such insubstantial entities as sensory data and concepts in minds. I suspect that it could be so only in the same sort of way as Wagner's *Ring* corresponds to the grooves in the discs that are a recording of it. We have, I believe, most of us, become enmeshed in altogether the wrong metaphor, the metaphor of a picture, when we should be using that of a tool. Wittgenstein came to this conclusion with regard to language, but not with regard to epistemology or so-called direct perception. Vaihinger clearly anticipated Wittgenstein when he said: 'This conceptual world is not a *picture* of the actual world but an *instrument* for grasping and subjectively understanding that world.'[1] But the point goes deeper. The most important error we characteristically make on every level about the nature of reality is that we mistake the instruments we have evolved for coping with it for pictures of it. This goes for direct perception as well as for conceptual thought. There are at least three ways in which we systematically make the same mistake: sensory, conceptual and linguistic. There can be no intelligible sense in which reality is 'like' the grasp we have of it, and still less 'like' the instruments we possess for grasping it.

One might have supposed that after Kant there would be no need to say this. But the great tragedy of philosophy in the English-speaking world during these last two hundred years is that it has never properly taken Kant on board. The approach to philosophy inaugurated by him achieved influence in these parts chiefly through the transmogrification it had undergone from Hegel – and when eventually that was rejected, the whole tradition it was thought to represent was seen as discredited. But the truth is that Kant and Schopenhauer, both of them better philosophers than Hegel, were never metabolized into the bloodstream of Anglo-Saxon philosophy. It is characteristic that the best known history of Western philosophy in the English language, Bertrand Russell's, embodies a radical misunderstanding and undervaluation of them both. In personal dealings with professional philosophers throughout adult life I have commonly encountered a failure to understand even what sort of philosopher Schopenhauer is: he is widely supposed to be portentous, inflated, boring, attempting to express the inexpressible – the same kind of philosopher as Hegel, in fact. The great – and it is a truly great – tradition of the past to which most professional philosophers in the English-speaking world

[1] H. Vaihinger, *The Philosophy of 'As If'*, 63.

24

still see themselves as most closely related is that of Empiricism. And I am afraid that for this reason they are still mis-taking our experience of reality for reality – in fact they frequently use 'experience' and 'the world' as interchangeable concepts. Radically and systematically, they mis-take epistemological entities for ontological ones. And on the basis of this mistake on their own part they scornfully misrepresent philosophers like Kant and Schopenhauer as saying that we human beings synthesize reality in our heads, when what those other philosophers are saying is the direct opposite, namely that reality exists independently of us and our experience of it, and must be categorially unlike our experience. All along, I am afraid, it has been the empiricism-oriented philosophers who have been confusing reality with what we synthesize in our heads.

Another fundamental issue raised by your question: 'How do I know that I am blind?' concerns our knowledge – or rather our ignorance – not only of the natural world but of ourselves.

It has always puzzled me that we do not know what we are. Millions of Christians, some of them of the highest intelligence and given to reflecting deeply on these matters, have sincerely believed that each of us is in essence a soul that will survive the disintegration of its temporary bodily home and continue in individual existence eternally. Millions of non-religious people, some equally intelligent and reflective, have believed, and with equal sincerity, that we are nothing but the matter we stand up in, and that when our bodies die it will be the permanent end of us as individuals. Millions of members of religions other than Christianity – in each case some of them highly intelligent, broadly learned and deeply wise – have held a variety of other beliefs that are incompatible with both of these, and also with one another. Whichever is right, if any of them is, the majority must be wrong. So as a species we humans are at the very least ignorant, and often positively mistaken, about what we ourselves are. And I ask how this is possible. How can a conscious, self-aware being *be* something and yet not know what that something is? We *are* ourselves, and a closer relationship than that of identity is not conceivable, if indeed identity can be thought of as a relationship. How then is it possible for us not to know what *what we are* is? How, in something self-aware, can possession of an identity be compatible with ignorance of what that identity is? And what would have to be the case for us to be able to acquire the necessary knowledge?

For many years I supposed that the key to this enigma must have something to do with the nature of being, or at least of human being. I now think that I was looking for the solution in the wrong place, and that it has to do with the nature of knowing. For me, at least, your situation has cast light on this question. You are blind, yet you would have no way of knowing that you were, or even of attaching any significance to the concept, if everyone else was blind also. Even as things are, I want to argue that although you know *that* you are blind, you do not and cannot fully understand what it is to be blind, what being blind consists in, because you have no experiential knowledge of the sense you lack.

Referring to the fact that, for us to be able to draw a line, we have to be able to see on both sides of it, Wittgenstein once wrote that for us to be able to draw a line *even in thought* we have to be able to *think* on both sides of it. Now there can be no identity without limits, and to understand our own identity we should have to be able to think on both sides of its limits; we should have to be able to see our limitations from without, from beyond them, as well as from inside them – and of course this is inherently impossible. From this it follows that no finite creature can understand its own nature. I am led to this conclusion by reflection on your letter, and I am coming to think that it must be true not only in the profoundest metaphysical sense but even from a mundane and everyday point of view. If on just one occasion I could see myself from outside as others see me – if, for instance, I could sit in a railway compartment opposite someone identical with myself – I am sure I would perceive all sorts of things about this person that I have never realized, and no doubt some of them would shake me, and possibly some of them would go deep. But as matters stand these are things I shall never know – or at least never know in the way I would if I had had the experience of seeing them for myself, as those around me constantly do. Even audio and visual recordings of oneself are notoriously surprising and disconcerting when first encountered, and these are mere echoes and shadows. Usually, when people hear a sound recording of their own voice for the first time, it sounds like the voice of a stranger. And when people see themselves for the first time on film or video they are usually quite seriously put out.

It may be that in bringing up such large questions so soon I am forging ahead too quickly – perhaps we shall be better placed to deal with these if we first address ourselves to other questions, also important but intermediate. But – whether you want to comment on them yet or not – I hereby serve notice on you that among my ulterior motives in initiating this correspondence was the hope that we might increase our understanding of the human condition *as such*, especially on the question of our intelligibility to ourselves; and this I find myself already beginning to do.

You end your letter by asking if I agree with you that blind people can understand the meaning of visual terms to a major extent even if not wholly; and, if I do, what I would say about that part of the meaning of such terms that blind people cannot share.

I have to say that I do not believe that blind people can understand visual terms to a *major* extent, though you demonstrate impressively that they can do so to *some* extent. What is central here is the distinction between 'knowing' and 'knowing about' or 'knowing that'. If I ask you: 'Do you know President Bush?' you would answer: 'No.' But you may very well know an enormous amount *about* President Bush. You could have taken an active interest over many years in contemporary American politics, and read all the available biographies of Bush, plus other people's accounts of events in which he played an important role, together with their memoirs of him, and assessments of his character and personality. You could have a detailed knowledge about the man which was enough in itself to fill volumes, but without knowing the man. The difference between these two forms of knowledge is of fundamental significance in life, as it is in philosophy. The latter is sometimes called 'conceptual knowledge' or 'propositional knowledge', because it can be encapsulated in concepts and communicated in propositions. The former is a matter of direct experience, which language can never communicate adequately, and often cannot communicate at all. Every experience is unique to the person, the moment and the occasion; and every existent entity is also unique; so any attempt to capture either of them in concepts, whether for purposes of storage or communication, compels us to abstract their general features from what is uniquely particular, and limit ourselves to conveying those. And however fine-cut these general features may be, however closely characterized, they must of necessity omit what is *uniquely* particular, for concepts have to be inter-subjectively understandable if they are to perform their function, and they need therefore to have a certain character of generality.

The point can be illustrated simply. There would be no way in which, to someone who had never tasted coffee, you could describe it in such a way that he would *actually know* how it tasted. You could narrow down its characteristics for him in innumerable ways: you could tell him that it is a liquid, usually drunk hot, somehow brown in taste as well as in colour (unlike tea, which is brown in colour but not in taste), aromatic, pungent and with a slight touch of acridity, full-bodied, giving a thick feeling in the mouth, satisfying, with a powerful and long-lasting aftertaste; and so on and so forth. And at the end of your description he would certainly know a lot of things about coffee. But how it tasted would not be one of them. No matter how many adjectives you piled on, it would always be possible that they might also apply to some other beverage – indeed, if they could not they would not be appropriate concepts. So your description would remain permanently like *Hamlet* without the Prince of Denmark: what was central to its purpose would always be absent, namely the putting of the other person in possession of the knowledge of how coffee tastes – as against, and differently from, any other drink. There is only one way in which he can find that out, and that is by tasting coffee. Once he has done that, propositions referring to its taste will acquire specific meaning for him, but only then. You will then be able to say of other things too – chocolate, ice-cream, cake – that they taste of coffee, and he will know what you mean. You will be able to introduce all sorts of refinements and particularizations now, such as 'has a weak-coffee taste' or 'has the taste of strong black coffee with too much sugar in it', and again he will know what you mean. But before the basic predicate 'has the taste of coffee' can have any experiential significance for him at all he needs first to have tasted coffee.

This means that any predicate about coffee that requires a knowledge of its taste before it can be fully understood requires that the hearer already possess that knowledge by direct acquaintance. And there is of course an indefinitely large number of such propositions. At the same time it has to be said that there is an indefinitely large number of propositions about coffee that someone who has never tasted it can understand perfectly well – for instance that it is a drink made from the beans of a plant that is grown mostly in the Western hemisphere and Africa; that these beans are first roasted, then ground, then mixed with hot water to make the drink; that the drink is taken variously with or without hot milk, cold milk, cream and sugar; that people tend to find it especially satisfying at the end of a meal; that it is a stimulant, and helps to get people going in the morning but also keeps some of them awake at night if they drink it late in the evening; that children tend not to care for it; and so on and so forth.

These two kinds of knowledge are possible with regard to everything that can be an object of direct experience. There is the kind that can be gained *only* by direct experience, and is therefore sometimes called 'experiential knowledge' or 'perceptual knowledge' – and sometimes, because there are philosophers who give the name 'phenomena' to the objects of direct experience, 'phenomenal knowledge' or just, in general, 'phenomenology'. Some philosophers, because of its apparently direct and unmediated character, call it 'knowledge by intuition', or simply 'intuition'. It recalls Russell's 'knowledge by acquaintance', as against his 'knowledge by description', which might also be identified with 'conceptual knowledge' or 'propositional knowledge'.

Now it seems to me that the whole phenomenology of visual experience must forever remain a closed book to you; that the only knowledge you can ever have about anything to do with seeing is propositional knowledge; that many propositions referring to seeing cannot be fully comprehensible to you; and that the remainder are intelligible to you only because there are people other than yourself who have a form of direct experience that is denied to you.

It could easily be that up to this point you will agree with me. And I must admit that I am surprised and impressed by your demonstration of how far you can make propositional knowledge carry you when it is everything you have to go on. And the fact that your demonstration is as brief as it is leaves me in need of no convincing that you could do more with it than you have shown. Nevertheless I attach two completely different orders of significance to the two kinds of knowledge. This order is implicit in their logical relationship to each other. The totality of propositional knowledge about the world is dependent for its very possibility, let alone its existence, on there being experiential knowledge: empirical concepts have content and significance only insofar as they can be cashed experientially in terms of *someone's* experience, though not necessarily that of any given concept-user. So the totality of empirical knowledge is either contained in or derived from experiential knowledge. On the other hand this relationship is not reciprocal: experiential knowledge is not dependent on propositional knowledge, cannot be derived from it, and exists in all its richness and fullness independently. The animal kingdom has an amazing range of subtle and refined experiential knowledge without, I take it, having any propositional knowledge at all.

It is itself an important consequence of the fact that the only knowledge you can have of seeing is propositional knowledge that you formulate questions about it in terms of your ability to attach meanings to certain words. I do not think it would occur to a sighted person to do the corresponding thing: automatically he would refer to direct experience. So when you make the claims to understand that you do (and I realize that these claims may contain a speculative element) you do two things that I contest. First, you disregard the fact that since vision-related content in any empirical concept must derive from direct experience, and since you yourself cannot apprehend such content in terms of your own experience but have to acquire an understanding of it indirectly by behavioural observation and inference, not only are you altogether incapable of under-standing some of those concepts but you are almost certainly apprehending only part of the content of the others. Second, by pitching your claims as high as you do, you talk as if the balance between propositional knowledge and experiential knowledge were different from what it is, indeed as if it were almost the opposite of what it is. Propositional knowledge, knowledge by description, is pale, grey, thin, second-hand stuff compared with the knowledge by acquaintance from which it is abstracted. It is the theoretical as against the experienced, paper notes as against gold. I agree wholeheartedly with Schopenhauer when he writes of the difference between them: '*Perception* is not only the source of all knowledge, but is itself knowledge *par excellence*; it alone is the unconditionally true genuine knowledge, fully worthy of the name. For it alone imparts *insight* proper; it alone is actually assimilated by man, passes into his inner nature, and can quite justifiably be called *his*, whereas the concepts merely cling to him.'[2] A person who knows everything about coffee that can be understood without

[2] Schopenhauer, *The World as Will and Representation*, ii. 77.

tasting it remains in ignorance of the one essential thing about it, the *raison d'être* of the drink. He is like a man who devours books about music without ever having heard any, or someone who devotes a lifetime of study to a foreign country without going there. Schopenhauer implies this latter image when he writes:

> With most books ... the author has *thought* but not *perceived*; he has written from reflection, not from intuition. It is just this that makes them mediocre and wearisome ... [But] where *a perception or intuition* was the basis of the author's thinking, it is as if he wrote from a land where his reader has never been, for everything is fresh and new, since it is drawn directly from the primary source of all knowledge.[3]

And again I agree with him fully. It is something on which I feel passionately, in fact, because all around me I see a failure to appreciate it leading to an undervaluation of sensory, emotional and aesthetic experience, and an inflation of the importance of the intellectual out of all proportion to its real significance; and these things are directly destructive of true values and the quality of life ... But I must not allow myself to be swept into that digression.

To recapitulate what I have said, but more tersely: I believe that because the only knowledge you can ever have of seeing is conceptual knowledge, and because you can never know what it actually *is* to see, concepts with visual associations can have only an attenuated content for you. You can learn about the sort of situations in which they are used, and you can become familiar with the ways in which they are most commonly connected with other concepts, but this is 'meaning' of no more

[3] Ibid. 72.

than a behaviouristic, black-box type. To my mind the fact that, according to some of the followers of Wittgenstein, your ability to do these things means that you not only understand the terms completely but can know everything that sighted people can know (a view that you do not, in fact, go along with) constitutes a demolition of that school of thought. It assumes that all knowledge is propositional knowledge, which would be a logical impossibility. Much if not most linguistic philosophy proceeds *as if* this were the case, even though it does not usually make its own false assumption explicit.

You, needless to say, are not guilty in that regard. Even so, from everything you have said to me, both in conversation and in writing, I infer that you vastly overestimate the extent to which you know what seeing is like, and vastly underestimate the difference it makes to a person's experience and his life; and this leads you to believe that propositional knowledge fills more of the available cognitive space in these matters than it does. I would put this down not only to the fact that you have no knowledge of ever having seen, and therefore cannot conceive what the impact of doing so is on the totality of one's experience: I would also guess that you feel no desire to do most or all of those things that sighted people can do which you cannot – for what is in principle the same sort of reason as I am not conscious of any active wish on my part to acquire a million pounds, namely that although it would transform my life if I did so there is no prospect of its happening. There are literally millions of people in the world who do have a million pounds, or the equivalent, and they are able to do all sorts of things that I cannot do and would greatly enjoy if I could; and yet in spite of that it would be untrue to say that I harbour an active desire to have a million pounds, or that I miss having it, or that I feel some sense of deprivation or handicap because I do not have it.

The fact is I never think about it. If I am right in the surmise that your attitude to the possession of sight is something a bit like this, then I suppose you are not particularly conscious of missing much. But you do, and the much that you miss informs that part of vision-related concepts that does not communicate itself to you. You surprised me a great deal once in conversation by saying that you think sighted people grossly exaggerated the importance of seeing. What I have just said points to the explanation I would offer of this remark. However, that is a conjecture on my part, and it would be an impertinence of me to put it to you without inviting comment from you, and being prepared for the possibility of rebuttal.

As things are, although you do not go all the way with the Wittgensteinians you still seem to me to accompany them too far when you imply that if one cannot say what something is then there are no criteria by which it can be asserted that one knows it to be so. I cannot say what seeing is, but I know what it is, and in normal circumstances I can soon tell whether or not someone else can see. You will remember that the opening words of Aristotle's *Metaphysics* are:

All men by nature desire to know. An indication of this is the delight we take in our senses; for even apart from their usefulness they are loved for themselves; and above all others the sense of sight. For not only with a view to action, but even when we are not going to do anything, we prefer seeing (one might say) to every-thing else.

The statement that we prefer seeing (one might say) to every-thing else gave me the shock of recognition when I first read it, for it is true, and not elementary so much as elemental. Part of my shock was with myself for not having raised the realization to the level of consciousness independently. There is something foundational to ordinary living about visual experience, and everyday moment-to-moment human interaction is predicated on the fact that this experience is shared, and such interaction could not occur as it does if that were not the case. Sighted people are aware almost perpetually of visual stimuli throughout the time they are awake, and their behaviour is so finely attuned to it, and conveys itself in so many thousands of subliminal ways, that I cannot begin to describe that situation to you: it is of the utmost complexity and sophistication, especially when individuals are reacting to one another face to face. The unending flow of congruence between expectation, behaviour and interpretation leaves no room for doubt, at least in most circumstances, that they are having visual experiences that correspond to one another's. If an individual fails to react, or starts to respond in ways that are inappropriate, this is quickly noticed. And that really is the answer to your question 'how sighted people can know that they have the same inner experiences of seeing as each other, and why, if they *can* know this, blind people can't know something about this inner experience too.' It is also the answer to your question of what the blind-from-birth woman who suddenly began to see knew that she had not known before. She began to acquire that whole world of visual knowledge-by-acquaintance that is incommunicable in words to anyone who has experienced none of it and yet is the seed-bed of all meaningful vision-related concepts.

From these multiple considerations it is evident to me that you as a blind person are unaware of the sheer *amount* of what is going on that passes you by. That in turn would explain your failure to understand why sighted people regard being blind as a cataclysm, when to the blind-from-birth it seems scarcely more of a cataclysm than our non-possession of radar does to the rest of us. But this redoubles my desire to stress the point –

harking back to an earlier passage in my letter – that we are almost certainly all in the same boat with regard to total reality: it is nearly all passing us by without our having any means of knowing what we are missing. It seems to me that the difference between what the blind miss and what the sighted miss must be as almost nothing compared with what we all miss. It is only by the Lilliputian standards common to us all that the difference between the sighted and the blind seems as huge as it does to the sighted. However, I do not believe it was this trans-cendental perspective that you had in mind when you said you thought the sighted exaggerate the importance of seeing. And given that each of us has no alternative for practical purposes but to construct a view of total reality in terms of such input as is available, and that the world-view common to most humans on that basis is what it is, the difference *on the human scale* between the sighted and the blind can only be described as vast. And the claims to understanding that you make can be made to sound as plausible as they do only on condition that you choose some words in illustration and not others.

What meaning can you attach to colour words like 'red', 'blue' and 'yellow'? What conception can you form of a game like snooker, everything about which depends on the differences of colour among various balls? What idea can you have of what a painting is, and, much more important than that, of what beauty in the visual arts is? For that matter, what conception can you have of natural beauty? Recently I was in Kenya, and visited a lake called Lake Nakuru. It has a high alkaline content, in which thrive certain algae, on which thrive flamingoes, a bird so beautiful that even my impersonal encyclopaedia describes it as beautiful. The lake is of a size that can be embraced in a single act of vision from a distance of a few hundred yards. So I found myself standing looking at a whole African lake whose shore was lined by over a million flamingoes. The sight was so breathtakingly beautiful it gave me gooseflesh all over my body, and I shall remember it for the rest of my life. What, I wonder, can you make of that experience?

Could I ask you to conduct a thought-experiment that might go a long way to extend our common understanding of this issue? I would like to ask you to imagine yourself in a similar relationship to some other person as I at this moment am to you. You say you surmise that the sense to which seeing is closest is hearing. Will you imagine that you have a deaf and dumb friend who has never heard any sound of any kind, and who has learnt braille so that he can communicate with you to the fullest extent made possible by language? Surely such a friend would be able to make all the corresponding claims about hearing-related words that you make about vision-related words? He knows that hearing is a sense, and he knows what a sense is because he can see and feel and smell and taste. He knows that this sense is mediated by the ears, as seeing is by the eyes. He knows that it is a sense that gives knowledge of the presence and location of matter, in its gas and liquid states as well as solids, and whether close or at a distance, though there is a much closer distance limit than there is on unobstructed vision. He knows that what is picked up by this sense is called a 'sound', and that for a sound to occur there has to be something that moves. So something moves and causes a sound, and this sound is picked up by people's ears and transmitted to their brains in such a way that they are able to tell where the cause of it is, and usually what it is, and very often a number of other things about it too. He knows that, in addition to the distance limit, there is a condition called 'noise' that obstructs the functioning of the sense. And he knows that when there are no sounds being picked up by anyone a condition prevails that people call 'silence', and that when they are calling for this they put their fingers on their lips, give wide-eyed sidelong glances, walk exaggeratedly on tiptoe, or make downward flapping gestures with their hands. Of himself he might protest that he does not, as others generally seem to suppose, live in a world that consists of this 'silence', and indeed has no experiential knowledge of what it is; nor would he know himself to be 'deaf', or be able to attach any significance to that concept, were it not for the fact that he lives in a world consisting largely of people who are not deaf, and who have inconveniently organized social life for those in possession of a sense that he does not possess. Chiefly what makes him aware of his deafness is the perception that others can do a number of things that he cannot do. Most important of all, he sees that by flapping their lower jaws and making various movements with their lips and tongues most people are able to convey to one another an equivalent form of the words he is familiar with in print and braille, and that this is the commonest form of human communication. He knows that by handling things called musical instruments, whose visual appearance he is familiar with, people are able to make sounds that are exciting to many, especially the young, and which others find satisfying aesthetically. And then, after all that, might he not claim that he is so used to encountering sound-related concepts, and so familiar with the sorts of ways in which they are used and the sorts of contexts and situations in which they occur, that he understands the major part of their meaning, if not quite all of it?

I would like to know how you would react to such claims? Separately from that, I wonder how you would try to convey to your friend what it is to hear? How would you try to get him to understand what music is, and why so many people regard it as the most valuable thing in life apart from other human beings? It is often said that being blind cuts one off from the world of things, whereas being deaf cuts one off from the world of people; and some say that the latter is the greater affliction, and that this is evidenced by the fact that more psychiatric disturbance tends to be caused by the onset of deafness than by the onset of blindness. I would love to know what you think on these questions.

There is one question in particular that I would like to raise with you about this notion of being cut off from the world of things. You do not actually put it like this in your letter, but are you not struck by the fact that sighted people are in some form of more or less perpetual contact with things in a way that you are not? Whereas you have no way of knowing what is around you, or where it is, unless you can either hear it or feel it, sighted people seem to have such knowledge nearly all of the time. It seems to me that this is implicit, though not quite explicit, in the examples you give of what it is that brings home to you the fact that you lack a sense that others have. They can weave their way through the people in a busy shopping street and turn straight in through the door of a travel agency. They can drive a bus along a road crowded with other traffic and not hit anything. Those are your examples; and what they show is that other people are in unbroken and reliable possession of knowledge-at-a-distance of the material objects in their environment. Does this not give you any sense at all of being cut off from such knowledge, and in that sense cut off from those things by comparison with sighted people? Or is it the case that because you cannot imagine what such knowledge-of-things-at-a-distance is like, you feel yourself to be fully related to material objects? In other words, is it the case what what you said earlier about the blind not, as the sighted suppose, living in a world of perpetual darkness has a parallel here in that they also do not, as the sighted similarly suppose, feel themselves to be cut off from the world of things?

The only person with whom I have ever even begun to have a

discussion such as the one that you and I are now having was Rupert Cross, who had lost his eyes in the same way as you, though I believe he was younger when it happened. He was, as I expect you know, Professor of Law at Oxford, and a Fellow of All Souls College, and was insightful as well as intelligent. One afternoon in his house on Boar's Hill I tried every way I could lay my mind to of conveying to him what seeing is. At one point I was referring to the fact that if the room we were sitting in were strange to him he would have to go round his half of it feeling each of the objects in turn to find out what they were, and where they were in relation to one another, whereas I could see all the objects *and* all their spatial interrelationships simultaneously without stirring from my chair; that sighted people are all the time seeing a large number of otherwise unrelated or only arbitrarily related things simultaneously, yet that this does not present itself as a chaos or a jumble, but rather as a synthesis of separates into a single picture possessed of some sort of unity. And it seemed to me at that moment, as it does to you, that the closest analogy with the other senses was with hearing. So the comparison I tried to draw was with orchestral music, especially of the pellucid kind we associate with a composer like Ravel. One may hear separately, and with complete clarity, yet all at once, the easily distinguishable sounds made by an oboe, two flutes, a harp, the entire brass choir, and 16 first violins, supported by a further string body of 44; and all the sections may be playing different notes; yet the result is not a cacophony but a single, harmonious complex of sound which – in addition to hearing each individual constituent within it – we take in effortlessly, indeed involuntarily, as a whole. Rupert thought about this for a long time, then said: 'I can't apply that to physical objects without a feeling of complete confusion. And I don't understand why it *isn't* confusing.'

The way he imagined seeing, he went on to say, was as some sort of 'feeling-at-a-distance'. As an example he instanced a college committee meeting, with himself sitting in the middle of a long table that had people all round it, with the Chairman at one end and Professor Brown at the other. The Chairman would bring forward some proposal, there would be a silence round the table, and then the Chairman would say: 'But I see Professor Brown disagrees.' What has happened during the silence to make Professor Brown's disagreement evident to the Chairman? Professor Brown did not say anything. Nor did he make any audible movement. Rupert Cross surmises that the only way in which Professor Brown's disapproval can have been behaviourally evinced is by a change in facial expression of a kind that he himself knows about and understands because of the movements of his own physiognomy that accompany his reactions, plus his lifelong experience of running his fingers over the faces of people with whom he is on intimate terms. But how can the Chairman know that Brown has done this? The Chairman has not reached down to the other end of the table and run his fingers over Brown's face – the table is too long, and in any case if the Chairman had attempted any such movement it would have passed in front of Rupert's face and he would have heard it. Rupert knows that the Chairman has not moved. So what he has done in some way is to apprehend, without touching, something that Rupert could have known only through touch. 'Seeing' Professor Brown's face is something the Chairman can do that gives him precisely the same information about Professor Brown as running fingers over it would have done, but somehow it is done without touching him. And the same is true, added Rupert, as far as the objects in his living room were concerned. As the two of us sat there, the other contents of the room were inaudible, so neither of us could gain any knowledge of them at that particular moment through our sense of hearing. But he knew perfectly well that I, without moving, could see every object in the room, and knew exactly what each one was and where it was, even though I had never been in the room before and had not walked round it touching things; whereas he, if it had been a strange room, would have been able to find out what was there, and where it was, only by moving around feeling everything.

I have now met two highly intelligent blind men one of whom makes an analogy between seeing and hearing in circumstances in which I myself have tried to do the same, while the other rejects it. Does this show that equally acute blind men have incompatible conceptions of what seeing is? If it does, would it follow from this that they have incompatible conceptions of what blindness is?

I think I have thrust enough problems at you for one letter. There are other issues that were raised earlier but seem for the moment to have passed into abeyance – for instance in your last letter you mentioned the apparently strange fact that 'blind people at least can hear objects, and thus make something of their surroundings, as well as hear sounds'; and in my last letter I wondered how you and I differed in the concept we have of a person, and in our conception of what it is to know a person. I have not mentioned either of those things in this letter, though we shall need to come back to them eventually. But it is impossible to discuss eveything at once. So let us not make the mistake of trying to. All the questions that lie before us now are fascinating, and there will be time to come to each of them in turn – and no doubt to a lot of others that we do not now foresee. I will leave it to you to take up those that excite your most immediate interest.

Yours ever,
Bryan

Letter 4

FROM MARTIN MILLIGAN
TO BRYAN MAGEE

Dear Bryan,

Many thanks for your second letter. I am very sorry indeed that it has taken me such a long time to reply. As you know from telephone conversations, most of the delay has been due to the pressure of practical work. But I must say that in any case I would probably have needed quite a while in which to work out how to respond to this letter of yours, because it contains so much; and because it has helped me to see more clearly than before the extent, and indeed the significance, of the enterprise we are engaged on; and has forced me to think not only about what I want to say but also about the shape of our discussion.

It is becoming clear that we are going to have to give quite a lot of attention to two different though related sorts of questions. And although discussion of the one group should illuminate and be illuminated by discussion of the other, it now seems to me that there might be merit in discussing these two groups in some degree of separation for a time. Thus, while the earlier part of your letter (from page 18 to page 34) develops the discussion of some general philosophical questions which, together with some of those listed on pages 3–4 of your first letter, will probably form the focus for the greater part of our discussions (and I am eager to come to them) I believe that I ought not to go straight to these questions. In the light of your last letter as a whole, it seems to me that I must first spend some time in responding to the views you have expressed, especially in the later parts of your letter, about the importance of sight to human beings, limits to the possibility of relations between sighted and blind people, and the limitedness of the experience of sensorily deprived people. These are not purely philosophical questions, but they do have to be considered by us, and you have said some challenging things about them which have stimulated me into wanting to say quite a lot in reply – so much, in fact, that I propose to devote almost all of this letter to these topics.

At the moment my intention is to go on pretty quickly, and without waiting for a reply from you to this letter, to write a further letter concentrating on the more strictly philosophical parts of your last one, dealing with such issues as the relationship between different kinds of knowledge such as 'knowledge by description' and 'knowledge by acquaintance'; the question as to whether there is any sense and truth in saying that some of our beliefs may 'correspond' in some degree to the world as it is; questions about self-knowledge and about human nature; and perhaps also the question of what it is to know a person. You could then decide whether you would like to respond to my two letters in a single all-embracing reply, or whether you would prefer to reply to each of them separately, or even to only one of them for the time being, so that our discussion would remain confined to one of the two groups of questions for a little before returning to the other.

Let me start, however, with two general philosophical points about which I am sure we are in agreement.

The first of these is that I believe, as I think you do, that nothing can count as human knowledge which does not in some degree and at some level enjoy support from, and therefore suffer from vulnerability to, the testimony of human sense-experience. In my view even those parts of knowledge which are formulated in the kind of propositions often called '*a priori*' (whether 'analytic' or 'synthetic') have a dependence on experience – even though sense-experience also has a dependence on them, and even though experience would have to be very much more different from what it is and has been to undermine *them* than in the case of so-called 'empirical' propositions. In my view, too, it would take much more experience, so to speak, to overthrow some empirical propositions than others. But anyway, in the battle between Platonists and Empiricists about the epistemological value of sense-experience, I, like you, am on the side of the Empiricists.

The second point on which I'm sure we agree is that in those matters where people have knowledge which has not at all been derived from, and which cannot be tested through, their *own* sense-experience, they may well suffer considerable disadvantages as compared with those in which their knowledge *does* derive at least in part from, and can be tested through, their own sense-experience. We agree about that, even if there is a question between us as to what precisely the disadvantages are, and how important they are.

And now with regard to blindness: here too let us start with what we agree about.

First, I do agree with you, despite the fact that this is not to me a self-evident truth, that there is such a thing as visual experience, the experience of seeing. And I agree, of course, that born-blind people have no such experience of their own, or memory of it, to which to refer. And henceforth I shall normally count people like myself, who lost our sight after birth but don't remember seeing, with the 'born-blind'. I accept that most of those who have, or can remember, visual experience prize it very highly indeed, and that those of us who are without it should recognise that we have been seriously deprived. I did not question this in my first letter, but only whether the lack of all visual experience renders us wholly or even largely incapable of understanding the meaning of visual terms; and also whether this means that there is any knowledge to which we are in principle denied access.

Second, I agree with something which I think you implied, though you did not say it in quite these words: at least some born-blind people, including me, don't often actively desire to see as such, although we do sometimes. Contrary to your surmise, I do frequently wish that I could do things sighted people can do which I cannot; but it is usually the *consequences* of having sight that I want – consequences which could in principle be obtained in other ways than through sight – rather than the experience of sight itself. And I agree with the explanation you offer of this, namely that like many other people (at any rate after they have grown up, and if they are fairly busy) I tend not to spend much time 'actively desiring' what I think I have no prospect of getting. Certainly, if doctors said there was now a good chance of restoring my sight by an operation, I would be actively interested (so would most blind people, I believe, although I have heard of a blind man who said he wouldn't); but I wouldn't have the attitude that I *must* have the operation, cost what it may; nor would I be bitterly disappointed if it failed. However, I am one of an extremely fortunate minority of blind people who have had the opportunity, and the special support, needed to undertake very satisfying work – as well as having good friends. Some other blind people might also not care too much about being able to see, but for an opposite reason – because they have had so little from life that they have lost the capacity to want much. Most blind people, I believe, including born-blind people, would very much want to see if they thought there was a chance. But I also believe that what most of us would be caring about to the extent that we did care would be chiefly the practical advantages of seeing. Speaking for myself again, although I would recognise that with the restoration of sight new aesthetic pleasures might become available to me, I would be too sceptical about the likelihood of my actually finding these experiences intensely pleasurable, and also perhaps a bit too puritanical, for them to weigh much with me.

Third, I agree with you nevertheless that blind people are missing a very great deal as compared with sighted people; and that what we are deprived of is not only an important range of practical abilities in coping with the world of things, and an enormous amount of information that it would be interesting and helpful to have (including many clues to the character, condition and stream of thoughts and feelings of fellow human beings, and a capacity to take in a relatively large amount of information about our immediate surroundings in a short time); but that we are also denied a range of experiences of a specific kind, some of which are to some of those who have them intensely pleasurable. And before you say it, I agree that the way in which, for brevity's sake, I have just put this last point is dry and diminishing. The way you put it in your letter, especially in your description of the experience of seeing Lake Nakuru, gives a far more vivid idea of the sort of experience which is being missed – an idea that would be wholly convincing to me if I needed convincing. No amount of words may seem to those who have such experiences adequate to expressing their content, impact and value. I can sincerely subscribe to the truth of this last point even though I have not had these visual experiences myself, because I *have* had non-visual experiences whose content, impact and value I feel cannot be adequately expressed in words; and because I believe I have good reason to trust you and others who say that some of your visual experiences are of this kind. I therefore agree with you that although blind people can understand descriptions of highly valued visual experiences, such descriptions, better than nothing as they may sometimes be, do not come anywhere near to making up for the lack of these experiences themselves.

Because I agree with you on the points dealt with in this last paragraph I also believe, as I infer you do, that blindness is a major handicap and deprivation. You would be wrong to imagine, however, that no one could possibly say otherwise. There are a substantial number of intelligent and competent blind people in the USA who support the views repeatedly propounded by Tom Jernigan, until recently the President of the American National Federation of the Blind, to the effect that blindness is not a handicap but just a difference, and that particular differences can be in some circumstances handicapping and in others advantageous, and that this is true of blindness. I disagree with that because I believe that blindness is a 'difference' which is so disadvantaging in such a wide range of frequently encountered circumstances that those who suffer from it should count themselves, and be counted as, suffering from a serious *general* handicap.

I also disagree with those who argue – as it has been fashionable to do recently about physical disabilities generally – that blindness is wholly or largely a socially imposed handicap. And, despite what you have said about the dependence of the awareness of handicap on there being unhandicapped people, I suspect that you and I will be in agreement about this too. For although many of the handicapping effects of blindness arise from the fact that blind people live in a world overwhelmingly populated by sighted people, and shaped by them for their own convenience, I would say that blindness would still be a serious handicap even if we blind people constituted the overwhelming majority of the world's population, and could arrange things to suit ourselves, and could subject the remaining sighted people to our will – and even if, as Wells has (perhaps rightly) surmised, we did not know we were handicapped. I therefore do not think of blindness as being *primarily* a socially imposed handicap, but as being a handicapping defect, by which I mean a lack or malfunction in the person who is blind which, in the present state of human knowledge, cannot be wholly compensated for or corrected no matter what society does or becomes, although its handicapping effects could be reduced and compensated for to a much greater extent than they are in wealthy societies such as ours.

I would go further still (perhaps further than you would want to) and agree with anyone who said that often, at least, blindness is a deformity – not merely in the sense that the eyes may be literally deformed, but in the sense that well-functioning eyes are, I am sure, an adornment which can give added life and beauty to a human face. In many circumstances they make possible a grace and effectiveness of movement which cannot be attained without them; and their absence – and the presence of poorly-functioning eyes, or dead eyes, or no eyes, with the accompanying clumsinesses – may fairly be judged (and not merely by sighted people) to be a defect in the form proper to a human being.

With regard to those points of agreement with you, however, I have to enter some qualifications. The first is that although I have agreed that born-blind people don't often actively desire to have sight, I would have to disagree with any inference to the effect that we don't have constant awareness of what we're missing. I don't say that you explicitly make that inference, but you come close to it, and I think it is relevant to say that the analogy you draw between the relation of blind to sighted people and that between you and millionaires seems to me defective, among other reasons because you don't live (I assume) surrounded by millionaires, with some of whom you are in constant intimate contact. Most blind people, including born-blind people, have daily reminders through their contacts with sighted people of what they are missing, and frequently experience feelings of frustration and of 'missing out'. Don't be deceived by the smiling faces and constant (perhaps rather wearing) cheerfulness of many blind people. They are the product in part of the good sense found among many people with serious disabilities of all kinds, which enables them to see that much that is good in life may still be open to them; and of the courage to resolve not to be a source of defeatism and demoralisation. But they are also sometimes the product in part of the desire to propitiate sighted people, by relieving them of embarrassment at their enormous good luck.

In any case it would of course be quite wrong to think that people *can't* miss what they have not experienced: virgins, after all, quite often long for sexual experience, and although you may say that when they eventually get it this experience doesn't always turn out to be what they expected, it would be unplausible to say that they never have any notion beforehand of what they are missing.

My second reservation is that I can't agree with you that if all human beings were without the power of sight 'the very concept "sight" would not then be able to exist', that the word 'sight' would be like 'scridge' to all of us, and that we would have no sense of lacking anything. As I have already indicated, I think that might well be the case, but I don't see that it must be. It seems to me possible that even if the whole of humanity were and always had been blind we would not necessarily have been stupid or incurious, and we might sooner or later have discovered electricity and radio waves, and ways of generating them. Perhaps in the course of trying to invent something else we might also have accidentally invented instruments which sonically recorded the presence of light waves, that is of waves which were akin to, but different from, sound waves and which we knew we were not normally aware of unless they were transformed into sound-waves by our instruments. With the help of these instruments we might come to realise that these waves were very widely present, though in very varying degrees, and were reflected or refracted by objects of various kinds. We might recognise that they could therefore help us in the detection and analysis of objects, perhaps even enabling us through our instruments to identify by sound those differences in objects which are perceived by sighted people as differences in colour. We might then have discovered that other animals have a faculty for detecting these waves, and for learning about their environment with their help. But whether we had discovered this or not, it is possible that we might eventually have speculated, as you yourself have done, that we could have had more senses than we actually have. We might realise that it would have been extremely useful to have a faculty within our own bodies for generating a specific kind of consciousness reflecting the presence and variations of these waves, and we might invent a special word for the faculty we lacked, and regretted lacking. It seems to me that if all this had happened the word in question would not have been without meaning as is 'scridge', and that it would have borne a concept indistinguishable from that represented for born-blind people in our actual sighted-dominated world by our English word 'eyesight'. (Whether and how far this concept falls short of the concept of 'eyesight' held by sighted people I shall leave for further consideration in my next letter.)

Furthermore, it seems to me possible that we might then have conceived of ourselves as handicapped compared with what we would have been if we had had this faculty. I don't say that it is *likely* that human beings would think themselves handicapped for the lack of a faculty which no human being had ever had, but I think it is *possible* that we would, and I even think that it *is* likely that we would if we thought that something could be done – perhaps by way of developing more light-using instruments, or by genetic engineering – to circumvent or eliminate the lack of the faculty in question. After all, part of the point of calling someone 'handicapped' is not just to mark an inferiority or defect but to indicate the need for help, cure or prevention.

So I cannot agree with you when you say 'You are blind, yet you would have no way of knowing that you were, or even of attaching significance to the concept, if everyone else was blind also.' Indeed, I cannot understand why you say this, since, as I have already mentioned, you have yourself said that we all lack a sense-organ for receiving radio waves, and you clearly think that these words of yours convey a concept of a lack, although no one has ever had such a sense-organ as far as we know. More generally, do you really want to say that no significance can be attached to any 'concept' (should this read 'word or group of words'?) if no one has ever had experience of what it represents? To counter examples such as 'black holes', 'a building 100 miles high', 'millions of years', 'a world without sentient beings' and, I suppose, an indefinite number of others, you would have to reply (I take it, as empiricists have so often replied): 'Yes, but these concepts – which do not directly arise from or refer to empirically possible experiences – have been derived from, or constructed out of, other concepts which do represent such experiences'. If I accept that reply, can't you accept *my* reply to you that 'sight' is a concept which born-blind people could derive from, or construct out of, other non-visual concepts representing what they *have* experienced?

So far I have been arguing only for the view that the experience of sight is not essential to blind peoples' being able to form a concept of sight such that they can make sense of, and recognise the truth of, the proposition that they are blind. The further argument you have addressed to me to the effect that 'although you know *that* you are blind, you do not and cannot fully understand what it is to be blind, what being blind consists in, because you have no experiential knowledge of the sense you lack' – an argument which I have not so far contested – and the related dispute between us as to whether born-blind people can understand to a 'major' or only to a 'minor' extent the meaning of visual terms, I shall again take up in my next letter.

Turning now to what is to me a particularly important part of your letter, covering roughly pages 34 to 43: the first thing that strikes me is that our discussions seem to be arousing more emotion that I had expected. You seem to have found my claims that born-blind people can understand, at the very least, a major part of the meaning of visual terms, and that many sighted people grossly exaggerate the importance of sight, somewhat exasperating in their presumption. I must confess to having wanted to protest rather vehemently against some of the things you say in this part of your letter. The presence of emotion, however, is often a sign that something important is at issue; and whilst it can make it difficult to stick to the methods of philosophy, it can also make it particularly worthwhile to do so. So: forward!

You say: 'You surprised me a great deal in conversation by saying you thought sighted people grossly exaggerate the importance of seeing.' Does your surprise mean that you think it would be *impossible* to exaggerate the importance of sight? If so, doesn't that suggest that *you* yourself may be guilty of some exaggeration here? But I hope I did not give you the impression that my view is that *all* sighted people exaggerate the importance of sight. I don't think that: I think some under-estimate its importance, and some get it about right. But I am quite sure that many sighted people *do* grossly exaggerate its importance.

What I was thinking of particularly was the trouble I and many other blind people have had in getting jobs for which we were fitted but from which we were excluded because sighted employers or their representatives had absurdly exaggerated ideas about the paralysing effects of blindness. To give only one example out of thousands that could be given from experience in Britain alone: there was a time in my life when, desperate for work, I was applying for jobs in Glasgow as a telephone typist on newspapers. This was a job that – at that time, at least – newspapers were constantly having difficulty in filling, and which I was well qualified for, having a good knowledge of current affairs and also certified high speeds and accuracy both as a typist and as a (braille) short-hand writer. I had already done this work successfully in another city. Yet although some of my applications were acknowledged, including applications for posts which were re-advertised, I was never even called for an interview. By chance, however, I met a man from one of the newspapers in question who knew about the trouble they had been having in making these appointments, and who told me that they had been favourably impressed by my application. When I asked: 'Why didn't you at least interview me then?', his reply was: 'Oh well, we just couldn't have employed you because there are stairs in our building.'

I have also heard an education officer explain that it would be difficult to accept blind children into the ordinary schools in his city because they nearly all had stairs.

Now, of course, downward flights of stairs *can* be a serious hazard to blind people who are on unfamiliar terrain alone, but most blind people learn their way around buildings they are going to have to use regularly within a day or two of first entering them, and they very quickly find ways of identifying where the stairs are and what these are like. Thousands of blind people in this country live and work every day in buildings with stairs, which, once they have located them and used them a few times, are no more dangerous to them than to the sighted users of the buildings. Not only were the schools I attended as a child full of stairs, so too have been most of the special schools for blind children which I have visited. Many sighted people, however, who do not know any blind people and who know that *they* themselves use their sight to locate stairs, and the distance from step to step, cannot imagine how blind people can do this without sight.

More generally, because the sense of which they make overwhelmingly the greatest use is sight, these sighted people just cannot imagine how blind people can manage without it. What they don't appreciate is that nature (fortunately) makes available to human beings a great deal of redundant information through more senses than one; and because sight is in modern conditions so much more efficient than the other senses, sighted people have got into the habit of disregarding a lot of the information the other senses provide, or can provide. However, blind people can learn to use this when they put their minds to it. Sighted people also under-estimate the usefulness of language. For all that you say about knowledge by description being 'pale, grey, thin, second-hand stuff', I believe that to be told that 'There's a downward flight of twenty steps immediately round the next corner, with a bannister on the right-hand side' is at least as useful as seeing them when you get there. And of course, many sighted people do not know about a lot of special aids and equipment now available to blind people. Given all this, I think one would have to be surprised if many *didn't* grossly exaggerate the importance of sight – and therefore of its absence.

I think it's desirable not to encourage or even acquiesce in such exaggeration, though, both because large numbers of recently-blind people are disproportionately depressed and damaged in spirit as a result of the widespread acceptance of this exaggeration, and because large numbers of people who at present have good sight are likely to go blind before they die. Loss of sight cannot, and should not, be experienced as anything other than a serious loss; but many people need not, and should not, experience it as the 'cataclysm' *you* speak of, because whether suffered early or late in life it can – if responded to with spirit, and with a bit of help from others – bring the discovery in oneself of new and encouraging powers, and the clear realisation that sight is by no means the most important thing in life. It is significant that a number of older people near where I live who have recently gone blind have chosen to call the organisation they have formed to support others 'VINE' – 'Vision Is Not Essential'. Some of us believe that this name has its drawbacks, but I think we all understand and approve of what they are trying to say through it.

You refer to my 'failure to understand why sighted people regard being blind as a cataclysm.' I can't think of any ground you can have for attributing such a failure to me. I believe that I do understand why many sighted people think of their becoming blind as a cataclysm; but I do after all also know many people who have suffered that fate, and I know that many of those who originally regarded this as a cataclysm have come to see it in a different light. I know that many have come to think of their loss of sight as not nearly as catastrophic as they had once thought, and that some have even come to regard the period during which they lost their sight, and had to learn to live as blind people, as a period of great net gain in their life.

In my last but one paragraph I said only that 'many people' need not experience blindness as a cataclysm – I did not say *all* people. For, just as there are many differences among born-blind people, so there are among people with sight. Among other things they differ, in my experience, in the extent to which their sight is important to them. One of my sighted friends, a philosopher, told me once that he thought he wouldn't notice much if he went blind. No doubt *that* was an exaggeration in the other direction; but nevertheless the truth was that he never talked about or seemed to take any interest in the look of things, and I do believe that he would have adapted relatively easily to blindness. Other sighted people I have known, on the other hand, seem to 'live in their eyes', as the saying goes: their talk is full of vivid visual imagery, and of information about the visual characteristics of things and people. One would expect the latter sort of people to suffer a great deal more from the loss of sight than the former. In fact, I have known a young blind woman who had lost her sight in childhood of whom it seemed to be true that all her memories of her life before she lost her sight were strongly visual – the colour of her bicycle, the look in her mother's eyes, and so on. That woman had learnt to live with blindness, and to work with much success as a blind person, but she never 'accepted' blindness; she never ceased to regret, and indeed to resent, her loss of sight, or to think of loss of sight as anything but a tragedy. For her, perhaps, loss of sight really was a cataclysm; and perhaps, given her make-up, it could not have been anything else. But I would have to say that she is not typical of the become-blind people I have known. Most of those who have been blind for more than a short time are very glad that they have known sight, and have regrets at its loss, but they are certainly not overwhelmed by these regrets or even, it seems, much preoccupied with them. Their minds are mostly filled with other worries and other joys. And even the woman I have spoken of – who, as I have indicated, represents what I believe to be a small minority of become-blind people – would not come near to agreeing that the loss of sight is the worst loss any human being could suffer.

That brings me to your quotation from the opening of Aristotle's *Metaphysics*, and particularly to the last sentence of the quotation, which in the translation you have used runs: 'For not only with a view to action, but even when we are not going to do anything, we prefer seeing (one might say) to everything else.'

Now I don't read Greek, but I have to say that I was immediately doubtful about this translation of the last part of this sentence. The 'one might say' looked puzzling, but I found it particularly hard to believe that Aristotle would say that we prefer seeing, the exercise of the physical sense, to *everything else*, because my understanding of his thought is that he would think that there are other higher pleasures, and that in particular philosophy, intellectual contemplation, can give a much more intense happiness than could any bodily sense. I have therefore consulted my friend Timothy Potts, who knows Greek and who has taught courses on Aristotle's *Metaphysics* for many years at the University of Leeds. He tells me that the

Greek is ambiguous, but that the passage we are concerned with can be translated: 'We prefer seeing (generally speaking) to *all the other senses*' (my italics); and his opinion is that this latter translation fits better with what Aristotle has written elsewhere.

But we are not primarily concerned here with what Aristotle thinks, but with what you and I think. It is what you say following this quotation which, I confess, has disturbed me a bit. You write (pages 35–6): 'The statement that we prefer seeing (one might say) to everything else ... is true, and not elementary so much as elemental. ... There is something foundational to ordinary living about visual experience, and everyday moment-to-moment human interaction is predicated on the fact that this experience is shared, and it could not occur as it does if that were not the case.' And, as the culmination of the whole passage, you say (on page 37): 'the difference *on the human scale* between the sighted and the blind can only be described as vast.'

It is my turn to be surprised – in the first place by the *tone* of these pages of your letter. They seem to me to express the passion, the zeal of a missionary preaching to the heathen in outer darkness. Only, of course, your 'gospel' isn't 'good' news to us heathens, for the message seems to be that ours is a 'darkness' from which we can never come in – not the darkness of course that sighted people can know, but the darkness of never being able to know *that* darkness, or of bridging the vast gulf that separates us from those who do.

But yours is not only not *good* news – it isn't *news* at all to us. We born-blind people already know very well the social disadvantages of not being able to make eye contact with people, of not being able to express ourselves by a wink or raised eyebrows, of not picking up glances, frowns, shrugs, starts, pallors and half-smiles which tell sighted people so much, of not seeing the glazed look that comes into the eyes of people we have been talking at for too long. We also know how much more quickly a sighted person can form a unified yet detailed picture of a room, as you described to Rupert Cross; and, even more striking to us, how, outside, you can take in at a glance the whole shape or setting of a town, and even quite small details of a scene which may be several miles distant – a picture that it would take us unaided many hours and much labour to build up. And we know that you are constantly aware of patterns of colours of which we can never be directly aware, and that you perceive much beauty and ugliness that we miss.

I think we know all that very well, yet we believe that we live in the same world as you, that what divides us is far less important than what we have in common, and that we therefore can and ought to share life with you, as full participating members of all-embracing human communities.

What surprises me in these pages of your letter is that they seem to amount to an emphatic rejection of this belief of ours. For if you say that, to those human beings who have it, sight is preferable to 'everything else', that this is an 'elemental' truth, and that 'there is something foundational to ordinary living about visual experience', you do seem to be saying that people who have no visual experience or memory of it cannot know what is of most importance to the majority of human beings, and that they just cannot share in 'everyday moment-to-moment human interaction'.

Now it is true that until quite recent times something like this was the prevailing view among sighted people in Europe and North America. It stills seems to govern behaviour in various parts of the world. Blind people have been isolated – pushed into a corner, herded into special institutions for the blind, and cut off from the mainstream of the life of their societies – not by their blindness but by the decisions of sighted people. Many blind people have accepted this as inevitable, and even pulled the barriers more tightly round them. But not all: even in the Victorian era in this country there were both blind and sighted people who thought that the isolation of blind people was not necessary or good for either them or the communities to which they belonged. Throughout much of Europe and North America, and indeed in many other parts of the world too, a large number of blind children today are receiving their education in ordinary mainstream schools, and in several countries the majority of blind people in employment are working alongside sighted people in factories and offices. Although in many ways practice still falls far short of profession, among both blind and those sighted people concerned with the well-being of blind people the avowed aim now, throughout the world, is almost invariably 'integration'. One never hears now open advocacy of 'isolationism'.

That is why I was so surprised to see those passages in your letter. They looked to me like an emphatic re-assertion of the old 'isolationist' view. Probably they were not meant to be that. But in order not to serve as a justification for the revival of what I believe to have been very bad old ways, they would need at least to be seriously qualified.

More important than all that, however, is the question of whether what you say is true. I don't think it is. I can't believe that it is an 'elemental truth' that all or the majority of sighted people prefer seeing to everything else, for that would mean that they would prefer to lose everything else rather than their sight. I think it can be true of very few that they would prefer to lose their spouse, their children or parents, their friends, their ability to speak and write, their ability to think and feel, rather than lose their sight. I can't even believe that anything like all of them would prefer to lose any other of their senses rather than sight: some would, but I'm sure many would prefer to lose their sight rather than their hearing – I know that many blind people would rather be blind than deaf, and in my experience most people who have both serious sight and hearing handicaps would prefer to have their hearing rather than their sight restored. I remember you yourself saying in your first letter that on reflection you thought that touch might be the human sense that it would be hardest to do without.

Nor can I believe that 'there is something foundational to ordinary living' about visual experience. Of course you could make that formally true by defining 'ordinary living' so as to include seeing; but I am sure that many sighted people who have shared a significant amount of their life with a blind person – and many now-blind people who have had a reasonable amount of experience of living both as a blind person and also as a sighted person – would not want to accept such a definition of 'ordinary living', nor would they accept that 'everyday moment-to-moment human interaction' is closed to those who have no sight. I do not believe that 'ordinary living' or 'everyday moment-to-moment human interaction' requires the sharing of any one sense. A common language comes nearer to being 'foundational'. But I think that, provided they have the material basis for living at all, if two or more people can each of them think moderately well, if they can achieve more than a bare minimum of communication somehow, if they share some common concerns, and something in common in the way of moral standards, and if they like each other, then they can manage 'everyday moment-to-moment human interaction'. They can also manage, together and if necessary singly, something that deserves to be called 'ordinary living', in that it encompasses a major portion of the kinds of pleasures and pains, hopes and worries, desires and fears, hopes, disappointments and achievements that are commonly experienced by human beings, whether they have a particular sense or not – even if it also includes some additional special problems, pains and pleasures not universally experienced.

You may ask what right I have to opinions on such matters, being someone wholly without visual experience of my own. Part of the answer to that question must be that an advantage which most born-blind people have over most sighted people in considering the importance of sight, and the relations between blind and sighted people, is that they are likely to have had more relevant experience. For whereas most sighted people will have known few if any blind people, and (if any) will often not have known them very well, born-blind people will usually have known a lot of other blind people, including blind people who have had sight, *and also* a lot of sighted people, and will have known some of both groups very well. They are also likely to have had more experience of interaction between blind and sighted people. For that reason – and also because an enormous preponderance of what is written and said in literature and the media deals with sighted people, and not with the blind – blind people are apt to know a good deal more *about* sight and sighted people than the latter can know about blindness and blind people.

To take my own case. In the close-knit family in which I grew up, both of my parents and my brother were sighted. All my early playmates were sighted. I had the privilege (admittedly rare at that time in this country) of being educated in ordinary primary and secondary schools predominantly for sighted children, schools in which there were some additional staff, together with special books and equipment, for the support of a relatively small number of blind pupils, but where, like most of the other blind pupils, I spent most of my time as a member of sighted classes: so I had close friends among the sighted as well as among the blind pupils. During most of my student days, and throughout the greater part of my working life, the overwhelming majority of my friends and acquaintances, including almost all my close friends, have been sighted. Of the women whom I have loved and lived with intimately one was totally blind, one fully sighted, and the third has had a significant amount of sight, although she has little left. My son, with whom I have shared much, has a lot of sight, although he is visually impaired. In short, I have had a great deal of experience of what I have regarded, and what I know *they* have regarded, as 'everyday moment-to-moment human interaction' with people whose visual experience I could not directly share – as well as some experience of living only with other blind people. This latter experience, of course, differed in some respects from the other. Blind people living together need more help from outside. At the same time, because they face some problems not encountered by others, they can form special bonds. But it is my experience that these are not necessarily stronger than bonds that can be formed between blind and sighted friends.

My whole life therefore seems to me to stand in contradiction to the views expressed in those passages of your letter. When I was young and did not get the sighted girl-friends I wanted I was sometimes tempted to think that this was because they were put off by my being blind. But when I saw the success some of my blind friends had with women I realised that my blindness had very little to do with this. Although most sighted people are naturally a bit nervous and tentative when they first meet a blind person, and although some have initially a tendency to treat a blind person as if blindness were associated with mental inferiority, or at least with insuperable problems of communication, I have found that all this usually wears off pretty quickly on closer acquaintance. Sighted people in fact often say to me, as I know they do to many blind people, 'Most of the time I'm with you I forget that you're blind.' This isn't the compliment it's sometimes supposed to be, since I see nothing to be ashamed of or embarrassed about in being blind, but I think it's very often quite simply a statement of the truth. When a friend and I are working together, or listening to music, or attending a meeting, or talking about politics or economics or history or science, or even about sport or holidays or people we know, my blindness usually doesn't come up, because it isn't relevant. Even if my friend tells me about the goal Gordon Strachan scored for Leeds United last Saturday, his description won't usually differ in any way from one he would give to a sighted friend who hadn't seen the match.

More important: when my blindness does come up, as of course it sometimes must and should, it's very rare for me to experience it as a barrier between me and a sighted friend – and also, I think, rare for my friends to do so. True, it *is* sometimes an occasion for problems between me and *some* sighted people. In the first place, I can believe that there may be a small minority of sighted people who are so strongly repelled by blindness that they fiercely resist forming relations with a blind person. I think I may have had one or two experiences of this; but of course it's difficult to be sure whether it is one's blindness or something else in one which is putting someone else off. Even where I have suspected that revulsion at my blindness may have been the distancing factor, I haven't thought that what repelled was simply or chiefly my inability directly to share visual experience, for my impression has been that people who care specially about their sight and who get a special amount of pleasure from seeing want to try to share that with blind people, and that their descriptions of what they see – although no doubt, as I have conceded, often seeming to them to fall short of their actual experience – are not only of real help and interest to me but serve to draw us closer. In any case, if blindness repels people, that isn't primarily our problem, but theirs. More troublesome, sometimes, than people who are repelled by blindness are people who are attracted by it because they see in it an opportunity to 'take over', to manage, or at least to patronise. If that were all that was present, the relationship with such a person would be relatively simple: it would be one of battle. The complication often is, however, that mixed in with these more doubtful motives there is quite often a strong element of straightforward kindness and good-heartedness. But in any case, what is at issue is, again, not the inability to share visual experience but the problems involved in the giving and receiving of help. That blind people often do make *friends* with sighted people shows that where there are compatibilities of disposition, common interests or just the right 'chemistry', such problems are not insuperable, or even often very serious. The differences in experience between blind and sighted people who are friends often serve, in fact, like other differences in experience between people, to enrich their relationships.

What I am saying therefore is, first, that although there are significant differences between blind and sighted people they need not be divisive, and are often not so. I also want to say, second, that not all the differences between blind and sighted people are to the advantage of the sighted, as the part of your letter under discussion seems to suggest. Many born-blind people learn to use their ears, their fingers, and even their noses to explore their environments to a much greater degree than most sighted people do. It's possible, at least, that on average blind people *think* a bit more than sighted people. There is also another difference, which I would like to approach through another bit of autobiography.

For the dozen years or so after I left school I had almost no occasion to meet any other blind people. And I had no special wish to do so – apart from one or two old school friends, and a splendid blind teacher I had had – as I was inclined to think of blind people as just ordinary people minus sight. But when it seemed that I wasn't going to get an academic job, and that if I was to earn my living I had better learn to do something that employers were already willing to pay blind people to do, I went to a blind training centre to learn to be a shorthand-typist. There, for the first time in my life, I spent several months living and working with a number of adult blind people, most of whom had lost their sight recently, though some of them had been born blind. To my surprise I found this a rather inspiring experience. What inspired me was the exceptional spirit and courage of the people around me. Perhaps it shouldn't have surprised me. These were all people still recovering from the trauma of loss of sight, or emerging from gross over-protection and sheltering, who were now faced with the necessity of learning to get about by themselves, and to enter or re-enter the ordinary sighted world. They just *had* to show a bit of extra spirit and courage. I think these qualities are probably present in slightly above-average doses in most blind people 'out in the world'. I didn't think of myself as brave at the time, because I had grown up as blind in the ordinary world; but looking back on that time from my present less active condition I'm inclined to think that I was quite brave too then. But I don't want to make too much of these differences either way. Just as there are certainly some blind people who are more perceptive than many sighted people, there are certainly some sighted people who have shown more grit and determination than most blind people.

So, although I don't want to under-play the differences there are in experience between the sighted and the blind, I can't see reason for saying that they 'can only be described as "vast" or "huge"'. At any rate I am sure that the difference in experience between a sighted civil servant in London and a sighted peasant in Tibet, or even a sighted miner in Kent, is likely to be a great deal 'vaster' than that between him or her and a fellow civil servant in the same office of the same sex and rank who is blind. And I'd be surprised if the differences in outlook and experience between you and me were as 'huge' as the differences between either of us and a Japanese, or American or even British millionaire, blind or sighted, who had made his or her money in cement, coffee, or the money markets. What matters anyway 'on the human scale' is not the 'vastness' of differences between human beings – the experience of every one of us differs a good deal from that of every other – but the extent to which we can unite in a community within which we can gain from and be strengthened by the differences between us. From that point of view the difference between those who have sight and those who do not is easily bridged compared with other differences between human beings such as differences of class, nationality, race, religion, sex and even age.

Now *all* these differences seem to me small, not because I have in mind the perspective referred to on page 37 of your letter, but when I consider them in comparison with our value and our potential as human beings, and also in comparison with what we actually have in common in the way of physical and mental abilities and social inheritance. I therefore agree with those who think that it is seriously wrong and harmful to lay great stress on those differences between human beings which cannot easily be removed or reduced, to the exclusion of recognition of what they have in common, or to emphasise superiorities that one group of human beings may have over another, without recognising the superiorities the second group may have over the first, or the overlapping ranges of strengths that there may be between the two groups – and without recognising that in any case such differences may be of little importance for many purposes. For that reason I agree that nationalism, racism, sexism and ageism are evils, even if sometimes inevitable and understandable. For the same reason I have to say that I think there is an evil which I suppose I will have to call 'visionism' (although, as I shall explain later, this term is sometimes used to refer to a different though related weakness), by which I mean here an exaggeration of the differences between the sighted and the blind, with a one-sided emphasis on the advantages or superiorities of the sighted over the blind.

I certainly do not think that you are a visionist. If you were, you would not have sought out a blind person and proposed a rational discussion of the differences between us, and their implications. But I would ask you to consider whether the part of your letter which I have been discussing hasn't at least the *appearance* of being a bit visionist, and whether you would want to modify the views stated there, by subtraction or addition.

I really don't understand why you should think a blind person would have any special difficulty in forming a conception of a game like snooker. As a matter of fact I personally have very little conception of this game, because I haven't yet been interested enough to find out about the rules, but I have a totally blind friend who knows the rules thoroughly, has played the game, and sometimes wins, he tells me. He presumably manages by the use of touch and some reliance on 'knowledge by description', of which you have such a low opinion. And I don't see why his conception of the game shouldn't be as good as many a sighted person's, since the function of the different colours of the balls can clearly be fulfilled if players (and 'spectators') know which balls are red, pink or black, and so forth, without necessarily seeing this for themselves. Before there was television they used to broadcast radio commentaries on snooker, as of course they still do on football, cricket, tennis, etc, so even sighted people must get a good deal of pleasure out of knowledge by description of such games, although it's obvious that those who can prefer to see them for themselves.

As to understanding the meaning of colour words beyond grasping that they mark differences in a visual characteristic: well, that and the significance of visual beauty for born-blind people are things I do want to tackle – but I think I must leave them till my next letter or later.

In response to the final pages of your letter: first, to your question as to whether I as a blind person feel cut off from the world of things. My answer is that I don't. I don't think that this is because I can't imagine knowledge-of-things-at-a-distance, for I believe that I can. Of course, as I have already said, I know that sighted people can get a very full and detailed knowledge of their surroundings much more quickly than can blind people. But after all what any one sighted person can see at any one time is only a very tiny fraction of his or her total environment. That fact doesn't make sighted people feel cut off from things, usually, and the fact that blind people can take in an even smaller fraction of their environment doesn't either. It's possible indeed that because blind people tend to use touch much more than sighted people to explore their immediate environment, they actually feel more in continuity with, more a part of, their material surroundings. When moving about, too, I think we probably have more experiences which make us more sharply aware than does sight of the solidity of many parts of the material world. Certainly the examples I gave of how blind people come to recognise that sighted people have something that they themselves haven't got are not examples of us feeling cut off from the world around us: we are all too conscious of the number of people, and the noise of the traffic in the street, of the rush and the bustle. What we know we lack is the ability to perceive the kind of detail which would enable us to navigate safely through it all.

There is one point of which I made brief mention in my last letter about which I should now say a little more. Born-blind people with normal hearing don't just hear sounds: they can hear objects (that is, have an awareness of them, chiefly through their ears) when they are fairly close at hand, provided these objects are not too low; and they can also in the same way 'hear' something of the shape of their immediate surroundings. Some blind people tend to make a bit of a mystery of what they sometimes call their 'obstacle' sense, but there can be no doubt about its reality or, I think, about its nature. Silent objects such as lamp-posts and parked cars with their engines off can be heard by me as I approach them and pass them as atmosphere-thickening occupants of space, almost certainly because of the way they absorb and/or echo back the sounds of my footsteps and other small sounds in their vicinity. It isn't usually necessary to make sounds oneself to have this awareness, though it helps. Objects of head height probably slightly affect the air currents reaching my face, which helps towards my awareness of them – which is why some blind people refer to this kind of sense-awareness as their 'facial' sense. Since an overwhelming amount of noise, and also profound deafness, seem to obliterate this sense, I agree with what seems to be the opinion of the majoirty of blind people who have it that this sense – usually well developed in born-blind people, less so in people who have lost their sight late in life – is primarily mediated through the ears, and should be thought of as primarily a kind of 'hearing'.

Different objects give off slightly different kinds of awareness. Thus a hedge which I am walking beside sounds different from a brick wall, and by this sense one can tell to some extent how high or low are the objects one is close to without touching them. For that reason it is not right to say that a blind person in a room which is new to him knows only objects that he can touch, or which are sources of sound. The moment I enter a room I have some rough idea of how large it is, and what shape it is, and whether it is full, or rather empty, of furniture. Sighted people have this sense too. Even with your eyes shut you would know whether you were in a largish empty room or a small crowded one. Even in total darkness a narrow tunnel would sound and feel different to you from a large open space. But sighted people usually don't have much occasion to use and develop this sense. Blind people do. I certainly don't want to claim that it's infallible, or that it's anything like as good as sight as a way of getting to know what's around, but what it does mean is that we too have a sense of simultaneously taking in a situation as a whole, and of integrating some detail into that picture. *Our* perception of our surroundings, as well as yours, does not usually present itself as a chaos 'but rather as a synthesis of separates into a single picture possessed of some sort of unity' – only of course the wholes of which we are aware will often be *much* more restricted than the wholes of which a sighted person can be conscious, our sense of their shape will often be much more blurred, and our grasp of the detail within it much less precise and rich.

I did not know Rupert Cross, but of course I knew about him and shared in the high regard in which he was universally held. I must say that I'm astonished that he should have had the slightest difficulty in understanding what you told him about the way you perceive a room as a complex whole, since I would have thought that that was exactly how he perceived it too. I have heard it said that Rupert was having some trouble with his hearing in his later years, but even so I should have thought that any blind person who had ever had reasonably good hearing would have had some sense of the overall character of his immediate surroundings – the sense that a room, and a hall, and a field would each have a characteristic 'presence'. Similarly, I'm astonished at his being puzzled as to how the chairman of a committee could know that Professor Brown disagreed without his having said anything. Since I can sometimes hear someone breathing harder or opening his mouth without speaking, I don't see why someone with sight shouldn't *see* these and other signs of restiveness at a distance: to know that someone has sight is precisely to know that he or she can be aware of such things at a distance without touching or hearing. Perhaps what Rupert couldn't understand was how changes in the optic nerve get transformed into an awareness of what is happening outside one, but that's not a special puzzle about sight: none of us, I take it, understand any better how changes in auditory, or, say, kinaesthetic nerves get transformed into awareness of changes in objects outside us. If that isn't what Rupert was puzzled about, I'm afraid I don't know what it was. My only explanation of what you report him as saying is that, as you say, Rupert was an exceptionally intelligent person who, besides being a brilliant academic lawyer, took a close interest in contemporary Oxford philosophy. Now, as Ernest Gellner pointed out in his delicious book *Words And Things*, it was the special achievement of Oxford philosophers of that time to be able to find puzzling all sorts of things that ordinary mortals thought were fairly straightforward. I can only think that

Rupert must have mastered this skill – and I'm afraid that I am a very ordinary mortal.

Anyway, I can see that it's a nuisance that the only two blind people you have talked to much about these things appear to disagree. I think if Rupert and I could have talked together we might have found that we didn't disagree as much as we seem to, but all the same, of course, blind people *do* disgree about all sorts of things, including blindness, just as do sighted people. I suppose that all that one can do is to try to take into account what different people say; to accept what seems to be confirmed by the greater part of relevant experience, provided that it is congruent with the world-picture which the greater part of the *whole* of thought-through experience seems to support; and if the greater part of relevant experience known to one *doesn't* speak clearly on a matter, to remain open-minded about it.

Finally – for I'm sure this letter is already too long – I should report that I have conducted the thought-experiment you very helpfully prescribed for me, and that I have found no difficulty at all in accepting the claims you imagine a deaf friend as making to the effect that he can understand the meaning of words like 'sound, 'music', 'melody', 'harmony' and so on. I confess that I was surprised at first, a few years back, when I heard about two profoundly deaf people who intended to make their careers in music. I am ashamed to say that I wondered for a little whether this was the same kind of silly self-deception or posing for effect which I have thought to be present in the claims occasionally made by, or on behalf of, totally blind people that they can enjoy paintings through touch. I *am* ashamed about that, partly because one should not be dismissive of surprising claims by other people in areas about which one knows little oneself; and also because I recognise that I ought to have remembered that there are ways of becoming aware of vibrations other than through the ears; that rhythms in particular, which are a very fundamental part of music, may well be very enjoyable to deaf people, both to perceive and to create; that perception of the structures within music, which should be open to deaf people, is for some hearing people a great part of the pleasure of music; and that some good hearing musicians get a great deal out of just reading music, without hearing it. If you were to reply that hearing musicians can hear music in their heads when they read it only because they have first heard it through their ears, my response would be that I'm not so sure about that. For me, at least, 'hearing' music in my head is often not like hearing through the ears at all: more often than not, when I think even of an orchestral piece, such imagery as I have is of what it would feel like to be playing it on the piano. Sound-images often play little or no part in my 'hearing', so I am not sure that hearing through the ears is essential to 'hearing' music in the mind, which is to say remembering and imagining it. So I now think it was a lack of thought and imagination on my part, as well as of knowledge, that led me to be so surprised, and initially sceptical, about the possibility of people who have never heard it understanding and enjoying music – although I think it likely that one would have to have had *some* kind of sensory awareness of music in order to be able to develop what we hearing people would be inclined to think of as anything like a full appreciation of what music can mean.

Perhaps I should add that, having had a little contact with one or two profoundly deaf people, I do not think that they are all by any means cut off from the 'world of people'. In so far as some *are* cut off, that is not the inevitable result of their deafness. It can, I think, fairly be put down to the refusal of hearing people (including me) to learn what I understand to be the beautiful and eloquent sign-language of deaf people, or to acquire other modes of communicating with them which, although slow, can help the development of close relations between profoundly deaf and hearing people.

But I am sure that I will not be able to get much further in saying what I think about such questions until I have more fully tackled some of the big philosophical issues you have raised, in particular the question of the relation between sense-awareness and concepts. Let me therefore stop this letter now, that I may the more quickly get started on my next one.

Yours ever,
Martin

Letter 5

FROM MARTIN MILLIGAN

TO BRYAN MAGEE

Dear Bryan,

Now for some of the more general philosophical questions raised in your last letter.

Your central argument I understand to be this. Human beings, you say, have two kinds of knowledge – 'knowledge by acquaintance' or 'experiential knowledge' on the one hand, and 'knowledge by description', or 'propositional' or 'conceptual knowledge', on the other. Knowledge of the first kind is 'knowing'; knowledge of the second kind is 'knowing about' or 'knowing that'. Knowledge of the first kind, you say, is logically fundamental to, and is generally more valuable than, knowledge of the second kind. Born-blind people have no experiential knowledge of visual phenomena, and although they do have knowledge of the second kind about such phenomena, in the light of which visual terms can have *some* meaning for them, the lack of the primary kind of knowledge deprives them of the possibility of understanding a *major* part of the meaning of visual terms.

I have to confess that I am not as yet persuaded by this argument. The principal purpose of this letter will be to try to explain why.

I Knowledge By Acquaintance and Propositional Knowledge

You explain your denial of the possibility of born-blind people understanding a major part of the meaning of visual terms by referring to the distinction between knowledge by acquaintance and knowledge by description, or propositional knowledge, a distinction which you call fundamental.

I'm a bit unclear, to start with, about your notion of 'knowledge by acquaintance'. You argue that to know President Bush is different from knowing about him. But for Russell, at least (the Russell who wrote *Problems of Philosophy*), knowing President Bush (except possibly in the case of President Bush's knowledge of himself) would *not* really be a case of knowledge by acquaintance, but a case only of knowing about, of knowledge by description, inferred from what we know by acquaintance. The latter kind of knowledge, in Russell's view, does not include knowledge of physical objects or of other people, but only knowledge of the data of outer and inner sense, memories of such data, and knowledge of universals. It is knowledge in which inference plays no part.

Perhaps, though, you disagree with Russell about this, and take the view (as I do) that there *can* be direct knowledge of people and physical objects. This would conform with common notions and usage, for we do talk about knowing people and we ordinarily don't think or speak of knowing someone whom we haven't met. People do sometimes say that they 'feel *as if* they know' someone whom they haven't met, but this just underlines that point. I think you were right in your first letter when you said that even if one had often spoken with a person on the telephone one would be uncomfortable about claiming to know that person, if that was all the contact one had had. I think too that you would or should still be uncomfortable about claiming to know such a person even if you had also seen the person, say at the theatre. You would normally, I think, only feel comfortable about claiming that you know a person whom you had met face to face and with whom you had interacted, or at least spent some time. So I agree with you that not all 'knowing about' is 'knowing', that not all propositional knowledge is knowledge by acquaintance.

But it doesn't follow from this that knowing isn't knowing about – that knowledge by acquaintance is a wholly different thing from propositional knowledge. In fact it seems to me that those are right who say that all knowing (as the term is commonly used today) is knowing about, or knowing that (knowing about, and knowing how, too, in my view, can quite properly be treated as forms of knowing that); that all knowledge is propositional knowledge; and that knowledge by acquaintance is just one kind of propositional knowledge. Not all acquaintance produces knowledge. After all, it's common in ordinary speech to say something such as 'I've met President Bush and been with him quite a lot, but I don't know him,' for even if one has met a person and become acquainted with him or her to some degree, one doesn't necessarily *know* that person. If one was too overcome by reverence or dislike or nervousness when with the person to have learnt anything about him, or if one simply doesn't remember anything about the person from the contact, then one can't rightly be said to know that person. If I knew President Bush, that knowledge would consist entirely of what I knew about his appearance, talk, thought and behaviour, his habits and inclinations, his moods, his different ways of responding to people, his interests, his passions, his capacity for endurance, his intellectual abilities and so on. If I don't have much or any knowledge of that kind *about him*, knowledge *that* he is and does, or tends to be and to do, such-and-such, then I hardly know him, or just don't know him. How well I know him depends entirely on what and how much I know about him.

'But all that kind of knowledge about him could be possessed by others who don't know him,' you might object.

Precisely. What allows me to claim that I know President Bush is not that I have some additional kind of knowledge they couldn't have, but only that I obtained the knowledge about him which I have, or some part of it, by meeting him and interacting with him, whereas they didn't. Knowledge by acquaintance differs from other kinds of propositional knowledge not by being non-propositional, but only by having been generated by direct contact with, by sense-experience of, its object.

'But,' perhaps you will persist, 'if you met Bush, you wouldn't just know about his appearance, you would *know* it.'

Is this 'knowing' anything more than knowing *that* he wears glasses, *that* he is of such-and-such a height, etc.?

'Yes,' you might reply, 'you would directly know your sense impressions of him, the sense-data he is causing you to have. You do not know *about* them – you just *know* them. When I spoke about knowing Bush as being a case of knowledge by acquaintance,' you might go on, 'I meant that this kind of knowledge by acquaintance was involved in, and formed the basis of, all the propositional knowledge you could acquire about Bush, whilst being itself non-propositional.'

Now, as I've indicated, I prefer the position I first attributed to you, the notion that if I meet Bush my acquaintance will be with *him*, to this Russellian view that my acquaintance would be only with sense-data 'given off' by him, as it were. But in any case this move doesn't make me want to change my response. Just as it seems to me that if I meet Bush, and in that sense make his acquaintance, this won't amount to *knowing* him unless I get to know some things *about* him – minimally, *that* he is in a room, *that* he sounds relaxed, etc, – so it is with sense-data, sense-impressions or sensations: my having them, and in that sense being acquainted with them, doesn't amount to my knowing them unless it results in me knowing something about them – minimally that I am having them, that I am hearing sounds, say, that I also have touch sensations of something soft in my hand, etc. And this knowledge is of course propositional knowledge, knowledge of truths, as Russell calls it.

If you were to reply that one just can't have sensations or sense-impressions without knowing them, that would seem to me wrong. Just as if I were very drunk or drugged I could meet Bush without knowing him at all, or knowing where we were – and without learning anything about him, even that I had met him – so, when emerging from sleep, say, I could have a dim awareness which was not at first an awareness of anything specific but which I later came to recognise as having consisted in part of, perhaps, pressure sensations in my back and a ringing in my ears. There can, I think, be dim, unspecific and unfocused consciousness which is not a knowing of anything, and therefore not any kind of knowing, and I think that one can have sensations without noticing or recognising them for what they are, and so without their being or begetting any kind of knowing.

But the main point is that whenever the having of sensations or sense-data *does* constitute or create or involve any knowing, that knowing is always a knowing that, even if it is only knowing that one is having sensations.

Russell does say that 'it would be rash to assume that human beings ever, in fact, have acquaintance with things without at the same time knowing some truth about them', but he does not explain why this would be rash, and his stated view is that nevertheless knowledge of sense-data, etc, by acquaintance is entirely independent of and distinct from knowledge of any truths about them. Of the colour which he is seeing he says: 'so far as concerns knowledge of the colour itself, as opposed to knowledge of truths about it, I know the colour perfectly and completely when I see it, and no further knowledge of it itself is even theoretically possible.' But what is this 'perfect and complete' knowledge? Does it consist of the knowledge that what he is seeing is a colour, or even just colour? No, because that would be knowledge of a truth, as would be even the knowledge simply that he is seeing something. But a 'knowing' which has been isolated from all knowledge of truths is not a knowing of any thing but a 'perfectly and completely' empty 'knowing' – a non-knowing. What we have left of a sensation when we take away all knowledge of truths or false beliefs which may be associated with it is not knowledge or illusion of any kind but simply the sensation as the occurrence of an event, as something which is 'had', like measles or birthdays.

Sensations do of course have some tendency to draw attention to themselves, or to other things. When I do notice it I may, for example, become aware that there is a ringing in my ears, and perhaps that there has been for some time. But the awareness that there is a ringing in my ears, or at the door, is a piece of propositional or conceptual knowledge. It presupposes my applying concepts to my experience and making the judgement that I am now hearing a ringing sound. The ringing and the making of the judgement are distinct events, and the second is a good deal more complicated than the first. The second is a piece of knowledge (or a belief – I have not been much concerned so far about the difference between knowing and believing). It may have been caused by the first event. But the first event, the ringing, whether in my ears or at the door, is not knowledge at all, though it can become an object of knowledge. It does sometimes happen that one has sensations of certain kinds and then subsequently interprets them as awareness that something is the case, but far oftener, it must be recognised, a direct awareness of a state of affairs, such as that there is a car going down the street or (if I may say so) that the sky is getting darker enters our minds directly, certainly as a result of what has assailed our sense-organs, but without any preliminary or even accompanying awareness of having sensations of any kind.

It's conceivable that someone might say on behalf of Russell or of the position I first attributed to you early in the present section of this letter that there may have been an old sense of 'knowing', perhaps preserved in the 'carnal knowledge' of the Bible, in which it meant *only* 'having contact with', without the least implication that there is any kind of awareness that anything is the case – a sense of 'knowing' in which this word would not belong with words such as wondering, believing, being confident that, etc. It might be said that if Russell or you want to use the word in this sense you have a right to, and that if 'knowing' *is* used in this sense there could be a kind of knowing of people and even perhaps of sensations which is entirely non-propositional. To this I would reply that of course it's open to people to propose to use words in ways different from their common use, with or without etymological warrant, but if this is what is being done with 'knowing' then it must be made clear that what results is not another kind of knowing, another species of the same genus, but another *meaning* of 'knowing'. The view I am supporting would be unaffected, except that it would have to be stressed that it is that all knowledge *in the ordinary sense of the word* is propositional.

'But hang on,' you might protest. 'There is nothing archaic or extraordinary in my saying that I know the thrill of seeing a million flamingoes on the shores of Lake Nakuru, whereas you don't and can't.' But in the ordinary sense of 'know', I would say, your saying that you know that thrill includes the assertion both that you have had that thrill *and* that you know that you have had that thrill; and, since I know that your testimony on this matter is utterly reliable, I too can know that you have had that thrill, though I can't have the thrill myself. If you exclude the assertion that you know you have had the thrill from the assertion that you know the thrill, in order to make your 'know' non-propositional, then you are using the word in a very out-of-the-ordinary way to say no more than that you have had the thrill.

'But if you have not had the thrill yourself,' you might say to me, 'how can you know what it is that I have had?'

'Because you have told me about it,' I might reply, 'and because I have had thrills as a result of things that have come to me through my senses, even including very occasionally that gooseflesh feeling you have mentioned.'

'Oh yes,' you might admit, 'I can see that the word "thrill" might not cause you any problems, because it is not a visual term. But how, for instance, do you react to the passage I quoted earlier on from Russell about light?'

Rather critically, I would have to confess.

The question Russell seems to be principally concerned with in this passage is that of what we mean by 'light'. To this question he does not offer an answer in so many words, but the last two sentences of the passage you quote imply the answer that light is a kind of sensation, and indeed most of the second paragraph of the passage seems to point to that as his answer – an answer which accords with a major doctrine of the whole book. But this answer does *not* bring out what we usually mean when we speak about light. If we meant by 'light' some kinds of sensations, how could we say, as we commonly do, such things as that sunlight helps plants grow even when no one is looking, that the bulb was burnt out because the light was left on in the empty room for days, that light comes from the window or the stars, that the whole scene was illuminated by the light of the moon, or that the light is blocked out by buildings? In none of these cases could one sensibly substitute for the word 'light' a phrase such as 'a kind of sensation' or 'light sense-data' or 'visual awareness'. And although we do sometimes talk about 'light sensations', it is often to *distinguish* the sensations from real lights, as when a person whose optic nerve has been electrically stimulated in a darkened room says that he has light *sensations*, meaning that although he 'sees lights' the inverted commas are necessary, because (as he knows) there are no actual lights present. By the noun 'light' we – both blind and sighted people – mean something which exists in public space, and which can exist and have effects even where there are no sensations, just as by 'sensations of light' we mean sensations whose presence does not imply the presence of light. To identify light with any kind of sensations or sense-data therefore seems to me absurd.

As I indicated in my first letter to you, it seems to me that a satisfactory simple answer to the question of what we – most people – primarily mean by the noun 'light' is that we mean that which whilst being itself visible also makes other things visible to beings with eyesight. Unlike Russell, I don't see anything wrong or misleading in saying that light is a form of wave-motion, because it appears from the work of scientists that it is electromagnetic waves which are seen as light by beings with eyesight and which make other things visible. I don't say that is what we *mean* by 'light', because it is unlikely that the vast majority of the users of the word to date have known about electromagnetic waves, though a reference to such waves may well be on the way to becoming part of the meaning of 'light' as it probably already is for scientists. Born-blind people can fully understand the meaning of 'light' set out in this paragraph, and on countless occasions show that they can use the word correctly and to good purpose, as for instance when they take steps to ensure that their houses are adequately lit for the sake of sighted visitors.

I am not of course denying the truth of the proposition that sighted people know light whereas born-blind people only know *about* it. On the contrary, I would *assert* this as against Russell, who is denying that sighted people have direct acquaintance with light as most people use the word. But, as I have already argued, that difference between blind and sighted people is not, as such, a difference in the kind or amount of knowledge possessed about light, but only a difference in the way it has come to be possessed. Sighted people know that light is itself visible and makes other things visible, in part at least because they have themselves seen light and seen other things by means of light. As I argued in my last letter, blind people *could* conceivably have come to know such truths by inference without any contribution by sighted people, but in actual fact blind people know these truths because of what sighted people have told them. Far from sighted people being unable to describe their experience of seeing light and other things, it is because they have described these experiences on innumerable occasions that born-blind people know about light.

You say: 'I cannot say what seeing is, but I know what it is.'

But you *can* say what seeing is. You *could* say, with me, that it is a form of sense-awareness available, where there is light, to beings with properly-functioning eyes and brains. You *have* in fact said in the very same letter that, for those who have it, seeing is the source of an almost perpetual flow of stimuli of very great complexity which conveys an enormous amount of information not only about the outward appearance of people and things but also about the inner life of other people; that it enables those who are capable of it to acquire very rapidly a picture of their environment which is both very detailed and yet highly structured; and that it is frequently a source of intense pleasure. I indicated in my first letter the sort of reasons blind people have for giving credence to the claims sighted people make about seeing: your testimony is so well supported by the direct and indirect testimony of so many others whom there is also good reason to trust that I think I have a right to say not just that I believe what you say but that I know it to be true, and therefore that I know these things about sight which you know and have told me.

It is very important to add that born-blind people generally do not know as much about seeing as sighted people do, but this is *not* because some part of what sighted people know is in principle inaccessible to blind people but simply because those who have prolonged experience of a condition are, if their brains are not too damaged, likely to acquire a great deal more information about the condition than can be acquired by those who have no direct experience of it.

In my last letter I mentioned that in my view there could be big advantages in gaining knowledge about particular things or kinds of things through one's own experience. As I've already indicated, these *don't* for me include being able to know truths that just couldn't become known to those who have no experience of their own of the things in question. Nor is perception *always* superior to knowledge inferred or transmitted by description in reliability, accuracy or relevance, although it often is. However, truths that come to one through one's own experience very often come to one with more force, with a greater impact, than would the same truths reached only by inference or through descriptions by others of *their* experience. Perception, and especially visual perception, almost invariably gives people much more knowledge in a given period of time than they could get in the same time from listening to or reading reports: perception 'floods one with knowledge', as I think Professor Armstrong has said. It also often make things easier to understand. It often offers one much more knowledge than one could have reached by inference and more than anyone would think to transmit by description. It permits relatively rapid, detailed cross-questioning by the perceiver of the information being received, not only at the moment of its reception but also afterwards, through the scrutiny of one's memory, or through new acts of perception. That is why, if one has had a lot of experience of a certain kind of object or process or condition, one is very likely to know a great deal more about it than if one has had little or no experience of one's own of it, even if one has been told or has thought a lot about it. People also often, and reasonably, feel greater confidence in beliefs which they have acquired in part at least through their own experience, and – although this is a different it is also an important point – are often and reasonably more ready to believe the testimony of others whose reliability they have established to some extent by their own experience.

Therefore, just as blind people are the experts on what it is to be blind – and I do think it would be surprising if any sighted person were to understand more fully than someone who has been blind for any length of time what it is to be blind – so sighted people are the experts on what it is to be sighted. But in both cases the non-experts can learn from the experts. There is no impassable barrier.

'But,' I can imagine you objecting, 'if you admit that sighted people have had the experience of seeing light and born-blind people haven't; and if you also admit, as you did in your last letter, that some experiences cannot be adequately conveyed in words, and that this may be true of some visual experiences; why can't you admit that the experience of seeing light may be an experience of this kind?'

I do admit this. To be precise, I admit that though description can communicate the *knowledge* yielded by an experience it cannot usually reproduce in the receivers of the description the full *experience*, or in many cases any part of the experience which yielded the knowledge. Born-blind people have not enjoyed or suffered, and cannot enjoy or suffer, the visual experiences that sighted people have, although (with one qualification to be made later) they can have all the knowledge that such experiences yield – both all the knowledge about the objects experienced and also all the knowledge about the experiences themselves. For the knowledge yielded by an experience is not, even for those who have the experience, a total reproduction, a complete recreation, of the experience itself, any more than knowledge of a physical object is a total reproduction of the object. I am suggesting that blind people can have the same knowledge as sighted people, but not that they can have the same experience.

But isn't experience knowledge? 'Experience' is an ambiguous word. It *is* sometimes used as a synonym for 'knowledge by acquaintance' or 'experiential knowledge' in the sense of propositional knowledge arising directly (non-inferentially) from the application of concepts to the 'manifold of sense', to the data of outer and inner sense. But it is also sometimes used to refer to that manifold itself – to the sensations and sense-impressions, images, feelings, inclinations, impulses, etc, which, I have argued, are not themselves instances of knowing, but which play a role in the generation of knowledge of other things, and also of themselves. That is why, for instance, it can be ambiguous for someone to say that he or she takes drugs for the sake of the experience to be gained. What is meant could be *either* that drugs are being taken so as to gain knowledge of their effects, *or* that they are being taken so as to enjoy the sensations and feelings which they induce. It is of course with 'experience' in the second, non-cognitive sense that I am contrasting knowledge. Even for those whose experience in this sense has yielded it, knowledge of experience is not the same as the experience of which it is the knowledge. That it cannot of itself wholly reproduce that experience is shown by, for instance, the fact that drug-takers who have known from their own experience the joys of taking drugs are not content with this knowledge but frequently wish to renew the experience (in the non-cognitive sense) by taking more drugs.

So when I claim that born-blind people can know all that sighted people know, but allow that they have not experienced and cannot experience all that sighted people experience, I am allowing a lot as well as perhaps seeming to claim a lot. As compared with sighted people, born-blind people have missed out not only on a life-time of visual sense-experience, with all its variety, vividness and force, and a store of visual memories, many specific pains and pleasures associated with seeing, and expectations of many kinds to which sight gives rise: in lacking sight they have been without the sense which, far more than any other, I imagine, gives people frequent and graphic reminders in their everyday experience of the extent of the interplay of order and chaos, of structure and change, of the ubiquity of decay and of new growth, in the world we live in. I do hope that I can convince you that I believe that these are serious losses.

Nevertheless the claim that if they cannot experience what sighted people experience they can at least come to *know* what sighted people know is important. For knowledge – the knowledge that is constituted by the putting together of concepts and of propositions in a way that corresponds to how things are – is crucial to two things which are themselves crucial in human life: it is crucial to the fruitfulness of thinking, and it is crucial to human community. It matters that born-blind people can come to know what sighted people from their own experience know, and that sighted people can come to know what blind people from their own experience know, because it means that even if their experience is significantly different, the two groups can learn from each other, can follow and join in each other's arguments and thinking, can work together, and constitute one community.

But the assumption that all knowledge is propositional knowledge would be a logical impossibility, you say. Isn't it on the contrary just that which you argue for – a 'logical relationship' between non-propositional and propositional knowledge, in which everything in the latter would be 'derived from' the former – which would be 'a logical impossibility', since concepts and propositions can have logical relations with, and be logically derived from, only other concepts and propositions?

What *would* also be impossible – and this seems to me the truth in your point about the importance of what you call experiential knowledge and I call non-cognitive experience – would be for human beings to have any knowledge if they had only concepts but no non-cognitive experience, no 'manifold of sense'. For concepts, thoughts, are indeed empty without the manifold of sense, without sensory input. But the other side of Kant's famous dictum has also to be remembered – that intuitions without concepts are blind; that 'the given' on its own is dumb; that uncategorised, unconceptualised sensations and sense-impressions tell us nothing; that experience without concepts *is* non-cognitive, is not knowledge. Perception, experiential knowledge, is indeed, I agree, as I indicated in my last letter, fundamental to all other knowledge, but it is constituted from sensory input selectively attended to, organised, interrogated and interpreted with the help of concepts, and it is always propositional in form – it is always knowledge of, or belief about, what is the case. That is to say, it is always something which can be expressed in indicative-mood sentences – not something which necessarily *is* always so expressed, or something which can necessarily be so expressed by all its possessors, but something which allows of being so expressed by verbal language-users.

I insert the qualifications in the last sentence to ward off what I think is a misunderstanding which may in fact have played a part in leading you to deny the propositional character of experiential knowledge – the misunderstanding, namely, that to assert the propositional character of knowledge is to assert that those human beings and higher animals whose behaviour indicates that they know things but who have not the words to express what they know cannot really be said to know them after all. As I have indicated, that is not my view. I certainly don't believe, as you suggested I did, that 'if one cannot say what something is then there are no criteria by which it can be asserted that one knows it'. Because verbal language still seems to be a medium unrivalled in its range and flexibility for the recording, storing and transmitting of knowledge, for the checking by the application of explicit and universally accepted norms of anything that purports to be knowledge for compatibility with everything else which purports to be knowledge, and for the generation by inference in accordance with these same norms of new knowledge from existing knowledge, I think that it is quite right that we should demand of anything which is to be granted the status of knowledge that it should be expressible in verbal language. But that does not mean that I have to deny that a craftsman knows that such-and-such is the best way to get a certain result just because, although he can show how to get the result, he cannot describe in words how to do so; or even that I have to deny that a horse can know that it is getting close to home. Perhaps this misunderstanding has arisen between us because you are inclined to think of concepts as words, and of propositions as sentences, whereas I think of concepts as the ideas behind words – the ideas which get expressed in different but equivalent words in different languages, or even in the same language – and of propositions as what are stated in different but equivalent indicative-mood sentences in different languages, or even in the same language.

Someone might want to maintain that because even the higher animals have pretty restricted powers of reasoning (almost certainly because they do not have verbal languages) then, although they clearly have a considerable repertoire of propensities and abilities – partly developed in the course of their own experience – for getting information from their sensory inputs, all that should be attributed to them are proto-concepts rather than full-blown concepts; and that their knowledge should be called proto-propositional rather than simply propositional, for the same reason. If so, I don't think I would want to quarrel with this very strongly. But I would be very unhappy about saying either that non-language-using animals can't know anything, or that their knowledge is totally different in kind from propositional knowledge: first, because they do seem to have some knowledge of the same kind as we have, and second, because I would find it difficult to see how anything could be called knowledge – how the tests could be applied to it which ought to be applied to anything which is to deserve the name of knowledge – if it couldn't be put into words.

So, to return to what you say about propositional knowledge, I do not agree that it is founded on non-propositional knowledge, but I do agree that *propositional* experiential knowledge – that is to say, perceptual knowledge, that kind of propositional knowledge which non-inferentially arises from what comes to individuals through their own senses – is fundamental to other kinds of knowledge (including, I think, mathematics and other knowledge that is sometimes called *a priori*). But I don't think the relation of dependency is as one-way as you suggest, since how we interrogate, organise and interpret our raw sense-data is in fact enormously affected by knowledge transmitted to us by others, by knowledge inferred from experiential knowledge, and by knowledge less directly dependent on experiential knowledge such as *a priori* knowledge; and knowledge of these sorts seems greatly to exceed in amount and weight, in the minds of most members of modern societies, the knowledge they have directly acquired from their own experience, although any part of this mass of indirect knowledge can at any time be put into question as the result of the perceptions and thinking of even a single individual.

Another of your strictures on propositional knowledge which I am inclined to resist is that it cannot capture the uniqueness of experiences. Is that quite right, I wonder? Even if it is in the nature of concepts to be capable of multiple applications, don't we have linguistic devices for indicating that a particular concept or combination of concepts applies uniquely?

Nevertheless, you probably want to repeat, a description of an experience or of a physical object is never the same as the experience or object itself. With that I agree, as you already know. But I gather from your letter that you may not be happy with my saying a moment ago that the propositions constituting our knowledge 'correspond' with the way things are, or perhaps with my saying earlier that knowledge does not *wholly* reproduce its object – I think you might be inclined to say that it does not reproduce it at all. I am not quite sure whether you would want to say this last thing though, because, following the earlier Wittgenstein, you actually give the example of a gramophone record's relation to the musical score of which it is a recording as an illustration of the sort of relation that may hold between our beliefs and their objects, and I should have thought that these days that could represent a pretty high order of reproduction, a high level of correspondence. But you also say that a picture is the wrong metaphor for the relationship between human thought and reality and that we should be using instead the metaphor of a tool, an instrument for grasping or coping with things. That in fact has been a rather popular metaphor among various groups of philosophers during the present century, and I don't think that it is wholly wrong, since after all there does have to be some congruence, some 'match', between a hand or a tool for grasping an object and the object which it is being used to grasp. More important, maps and photographs, and recordings, do serve as tools for the explorer and other investigators. They can do so *because*, despite the fact that they differ markedly in size and shape, in the materials they are made of, and in many other ways, from what they repro-duce, there *is* a correspondence between them and what they represent such that study of a good map, to take that example, can help one to get a grasp of and to cope with the area it maps. Hearing a verbal description of the area, or remembering what one knows of the area from an earlier visit, would seem to perform very much the same function, just as having a good description of a person can function like having a good photograph. If there is a 'deep mystery' about what 'correspondence' 'can so much as mean' as applied to the relation between thought and the world, it would seem to be no more if no less deep than the mystery of what it means to say that a map or a photograph corresponds to what it portrays. On the other hand, when one thinks of tools like hammers and chisels, what strikes one is how different concepts and thinking are from many tools, which we typically use for the purpose of directly *changing* the external world, whereas what we use concepts for directly is to gain or spread knowledge and understanding of the world. The fact that the point of gaining the understanding may be to be able to change the world doesn't make the gaining of understanding the same thing as the changing of the world. It is true that the later Wittgenstein likened language to tool-kits, but of course words *do* serve other functions besides that of bearing concepts, and helping with the search for and transmission of knowledge. But for these latter processes the 'picturing' metaphor seems to me more apt, or at least less liable to be misleading, than the 'tool' metaphor.

Let us end this long section of the present letter with coffee. I agree of course that those who have never tasted coffee don't know the taste of coffee – that is to say, have not derived any knowledge they have about the taste of coffee by tasting it for themselves. From what has gone before you will know that my inclination, however, will be to argue, first, that it's not certain that all those who *have* tasted coffee know the taste of coffee, and second, that those who haven't tasted coffee can learn by description what those who have tasted it know about its taste. Our criteria for establishing whether someone knows a particular taste are of course different from those for establishing whether someone knows a particular person. We would probably be satisfied that someone knew a particular taste if he or she could pass a number of sensory recognition tests, whereas these would hardly do for establishing who knows President Bush. But what those people who talk about the taste of coffee *say* about it could also be an indicator of how well they know that taste. If someone were to say that the taste of coffee was very like the taste of lemonade we would have some doubts about what they knew about different tastes, even if we didn't have any sense of taste ourselves; because to say such a thing would be at such variance with much other evidence.

Now as it happens the question of what is the taste of coffee has been something of an issue for me in a very small way. I drink coffee only occasionally, and mostly what I have drunk has been instant coffee, or coffee which experienced coffee drinkers usually described as very bad coffee, which I nearly always drank with much milk and sugar. Usually I found the sweet, mild taste of what I drank inoffensive but uninteresting. But quite often I found what I was given as coffee to be simply unpleasant to taste – and this has sometimes been true of coffee that enthusiasts recommended. But since there clearly were many people who did get great satisfaction from coffee I have kept wondering what I was missing, and whether I had *really* tasted coffee. By an irony so beautiful that I fear that you will find it hard to believe, it was actually the very detailed description of the taste of coffee *you* gave in this last letter of yours, in which you nevertheless say that the taste of coffee *cannot* be described to someone who has not tasted it, which finally convinced me that I had never tasted it, and that what I had tasted was a different drink. The idea, for instance, that coffee had a 'powerful and long-lasting after-taste' had never entered my head until I read your letter. After I read it I determined to start drinking coffee black and without sugar, which of course other people had advised me to do, but which I'd been frightened away from previously by the acridity of the taste – not always so slight. Your passage persuaded me that a 'slight touch of acridity' *could* be something one need not be afraid of, that it could perhaps be part of the pleasure of drinking coffee. (I'm sure this sort of thing happens quite often: people who initially don't enjoy smoking, or the taste of beer, wine or spirits, persist in trying them because they know that other people enjoy these things, until eventually they discover the pleasure in them, helped by the descriptions of enthusiasts, which give guidance about what to look for.) So I have now had one or two cups of black, sugarless, ground coffee, and I do now recognise the taste – including its 'brownness', I think – which you have described. I no longer react to its pungency with such active dislike, and for the first time I begin to get some idea of how some people could grow to like the taste very much. Even so, I wouldn't say that I have come to find it deeply satisfying; but whether this is because the coffee I am trying isn't of the best, or because, as my wife says, my sense of taste is coarse, I don't know. It is worth bearing in mind that no individual can be said to know how reliable are the judgements he is directly prompted to make by what comes to him through his senses without independent corroboration.

Now of course, part of the point of my telling you this about my experience of coffee is to illustrate the truth of what I said earlier about knowledge by description playing a role in affecting the experiential knowledge one gets. Perhaps you will accept that. But I imagine that you might want to go on to say that, although your description of the taste of coffee did make enough sense to me before I had actually known that taste to make me recognise that I had not experienced it before, still I had to go on and taste the real thing for myself before I knew that your description was right.

But are you sure about that? Supposing I happened to have no sense of taste at all and never drank coffee, but all the same (perhaps because I was in advertising) badly wanted to know about the taste of coffee. Couldn't I find out everything I needed to know? Couldn't I try out your description on a large number of coffee addicts and find out if they concurred? Might I not carry out a large number of tests both on those who said they liked and on those who said they disliked coffee, with different blends presented in different ways, and note reactions? If I found a very wide consensus that your description was right, wouldn't I know that you had rightly described the taste of coffee better than you can know this for yourself; and if (as is possible) I found that different groups of addicts described what they regarded as the taste of coffee differently, might I not rightly conclude that there is not any one taste that is *the* taste of coffee, but several related coffee tastes? And if I found out why so many people disliked coffee, and if I had influence on the coffee trade, mightn't I make some recommendations that led to significant changes in the marketing of coffee, and in prevailing coffee tastes? Might I not in any case end up knowing a good deal more about the taste of coffee than do most coffee drinkers? It would still be true of course that I wouldn't myself know the taste of coffee in the sense of having had personal experience of it, but that needn't mean that there would be any piece of knowledge about coffee which I lacked.

I therefore think that you go too far when you say 'A person who knows everything about coffee that can be understood without tasting it remains in ignorance of the one essential thing about it, the *raison d'être* of the drink'. For the purposes of the present discussion I will accept that the *raison d'être* of coffee is that people like to drink it (although I think that the relationship between production and consumers' tastes is generally a bit more complex than that suggests) but anyone can know that a large number of people like drinking coffee, and can spend a life-time growing or selling coffee, without liking or even tasting it for themselves. So I simply can't see what is the essential thing about coffee of which such a person must be ignorant. Missing the particular pleasure that many people get from the drinking of coffee is of course something, but it is not in itself a lack of knowledge, since those who know and those who don't know the taste of coffee all know or can know that a lot of people have enjoyed coffee and a lot haven't.

Yet, you may say, there must be one piece of knowledge that people who have tasted coffee can have which people who have not tasted it cannot have – namely, that they have tasted coffee. Here I would agree. This is the 'one qualification' to which I referred earlier when saying that but for it born-blind people could have all the propositional knowledge that sighted people have. They cannot of course know that they have had sight, since they haven't, and they therefore cannot know that they have seen colours or anything else. They can know everything about colours and other visible things which sighted people know (though they very seldom do in fact), but they can't know that they have seen them. People like me who have had sight for a little but cannot remember it cannot know that we have either memories or experiences of seeing. Also, of course, people who have had sight all their lives cannot know that they have been blind. In my first letter to you I said that I was inclined to agree that there is something that people like me and born-blind people don't know, and sighted people and people who remember seeing do know, though I thought it was difficult to say what that is: well, I think now that it is just this – that we don't and can't know that we have experiences and memories of seeing, whereas sighted people do. I have been arguing that this makes less difference than people might think, but it *is* a difference, and in addition the difference in experience between us and people who do have experience, or at least memories, of seeing, as well as the difference in the amount of knowledge of visual things that we actually have, as against sighted people, may perhaps, on examination, turn out to have consequences for the meaning of visual terms for us and for you.

II Meaning and Understanding

In your first letter you said that we would have to dig into the intelligibility to each other of the difference between us that arises from having and not having sight. That, you said, 'will open up the whole question of the communicability of experiences to a person who has never had anything that corresponds to them'. I agreed, and that is why in my first letter I went a little into the question of what visual terms can mean to a born-blind person, or to one who does not remember seeing.

In that letter I suggested that, because blind people can perceive through other senses, they can understand seeing as a species of perceiving, and can understand other visual terms as representing characteristics of things either identical with or in some respects similar to characteristics known to themselves through touch and hearing. I was therefore arguing that blind people have non-visual experiences which do to some extent correspond in detail with visual experiences, and which in any case resemble visual experience in being informative, and which very often confirm or are confirmed by visual experience. I concluded that blind people could therefore understand a 'very major part' of the meaning of visual terms, though I did not think we could understand them completely.

In your reply you say that you accept that born-blind people can understand visual terms to some extent, but that you do not think we can understand a major part of their meaning. You seek to explain this view by reference to the distinction between experiential knowledge and propositional knowledge, relying chiefly, I think, on the argument that as experiential knowledge is non-conceptual and non-propositional it cannot be communicated to those who have not had the relevant experience. That is why I felt that I had to explain at some length why it does not seem to me that any knowledge is non-conceptual or non-propositional, in the sense of being incapable of being expressed in indicative-mood sentences. If I am right about this, then an important line of argument of yours against the possible meaningfulness of visual terms to blind people would seem to fall.

I might add that if experiential knowledge *were* to be non-conceptual, I don't see how it could be exchanged even among those who have had similar experiences, or how they could even know, with the confidence they have, that they have had similar experiences. I think I failed to explain this point clearly when I tried to make it in my first letter. What I was implying was *not* that people don't know when they are having or have had similar experiences, but rather that they couldn't know this without using concepts.

But in your letter there is also a second strand of argument to which I have not yet responded. This seems to be in effect that even if concepts can after all capture or recapture something of

103

experience, they cannot do so for those who have not had the experience. In one passage you say: 'You disregard the fact that since vision-related content in any empirical concept must derive from direct experience, and since you yourself cannot apprehend such content in terms of your own experience but have to acquire understanding of it indirectly by behavioural observation and inference, not only are you altogether incapable of understanding some of those concepts but you are almost certainly apprehending only part of the content of the others.' Later you say: 'Because the only knowledge you can ever have of seeing is conceptual knowledge, and because you can never know what it actually *is* to see, concepts with visual associations can have only an attenuated content for you. You can learn about the sort of situations in which they are used, and you can become familiar with the ways in which they are most commonly connected with other concepts, but this is "meaning" of no more than a behaviouristic, black-box type.'

I think that I should begin responding to this argument by trying to explain more clearly what I have in mind when I say that born-blind people can understand 'a very major part' but not all of the meaning of visual terms. By 'visual terms', first of all, I mean words which refer either to seeing or to what is seen. Next, 'meaning'. This is another of those very ambiguous words. It is common to distinguish a number of different meanings of 'meaning', and I think that it is right to do so – even if it is also right to say that most if not all of these meanings are related to one another by family resemblance, perhaps even as parts, specialisations or developments of one basic sense of 'meaning'.

For my present purpose I need to distinguish only two kinds of meanings of visual terms, namely what may be called 'conceptual' meanings and what may be called 'experiential' meanings. What concepts are, and even what experience is, are difficult and complicated questions, and I'm afraid that my exposition of these two kinds of meanings will be pretty rough-and-ready; but I hope that it will suffice to indicate the sort of thing I have in mind. By the 'conceptual' meaning or meanings of a word (for many words have different conceptual meanings in different contexts) I mean the concept or concepts which a word or group of words in a particular language expresses or represents for the users of that language. By a 'concept' I mean the idea or thought of a class of objects – that is to say, the thought of a class of actual or possible, physical or mental, things, processes, characteristics, actions or relationships, or of other objects of thought which perhaps don't fit into any of these categories, such as numbers or periods of time. Concepts (together with logical connectives) constitute the basic components of propositions, of what are stated in indicative-mood sentences, as these (together with logical connectives) are the components of trains of thought and of lines of argument, which always begin and end by asserting or denying that the objects of specific concepts either do or do not belong together in some way.

If someone does not understand the conceptual meaning of a word, it can often be explained by indicating the class of objects of which the class of objects represented by the concept expressed by the word is a sub-class, and by then indicating how this sub-class differs from the other sub-classes; this is often done with the help of other words. Most dictionary meanings are what I am calling conceptual meanings of words. Whilst individuals can propose new concepts or conceptual meanings for words, and new words for concepts, this has generally to be done by the use of words whose conceptual meanings are not determined by decisions of particular individuals but only by the concurrence in use of many of the users of the language in question. Whether the conceptual meaning of a word has been determined by consensus among the users of the language or by a proposal by a specific individual, once established, a conceptual meaning of a word has to be treated as being *the meaning of that word* in that context for individuals speaking the language, whoever they are. Conceptual meanings are not subject to variation from individual to individual according to the experience of the individual, or subject to variation from time to time according to changes in the physical or psychological state of individuals, for constancy of meaning is essential if words are to play a role either in communicating knowledge or in rational discussion – and it is to facilitate communication and rational discussion that words have conceptual meanings.

By the 'experiential' meaning of words I mean the associations and resonances words arouse in the minds of particular individuals as a result of their particular experiences. By the 'associations' of a word I mean not only the train of other words individuals may find coming to their minds on hearing, seeing or thinking of a word, but also the sensory images it may bring before the mind, the memories it may awaken, the emotions it may engender and the desires and intentions it may prompt. By the 'resonance' of a word I mean the often less easily described effects it may have on the emotions and other feelings, or on the moods of individuals. The experiential meaning of a word is always the *personal* meaning the word has for a particular individual; and although a word can have the same or similar experiential meaning for many individuals, meaning in this sense will often vary from individual to individual, and also from time to time, according to the state of the individuals encountering or using the word.

Corresponding in some degree to these two kinds of meaning, I suggest, are two kinds of understanding, which can be called respectively 'conceptual' and 'sympathetic' understanding. Conceptual understanding is of words, and is present when I correctly apprehend the ideas words are being used to express. Sympathetic understanding is of what goes on in people, and is present when (often as a result of understanding the conceptual meaning of words used by them) I remember or correctly imagine what other people are experiencing or have experienced, sometimes as a result of words they have encountered. There is a third kind of understanding, also related to experiential meaning of words, which is the kind of understanding possessed by some people in advertising, by some propagandists and by some creative writers, and longed for by some lovers: the understanding of how to do things to people with words. It might be called rhetoric-understanding.

Words are by no means always used to express concepts. Nor do they always, or perhaps relatively often, have a significant amount of experiential meaning. Even what are primarily visual terms can lack both conceptual and experiential meaning, as in exclamations such as 'Look here!'. It is very common to use vision-related words to bear non-visual concepts, as in 'I could see the force of the argument'. But even in the many cases where visual terms are used literally as such, I would say that their conceptual meanings can be grasped, and grasped fully and unattenuated, by born-blind people. Why should it not be so? As I argued in my last letter, we can all of us think quite clearly about classes of objects none of whose members have ever been experienced or could ever be experienced. We can, for instance, think about material objects existing before any sentient creature existed. Experience of what they denote is not needed to give *conceptual meaning* to words. What it is needed for is to establish whether concepts have application, whether anything corresponding to the conceptual meanings of words actually exists. Even then the experience can be very indirect evidence. It is certainly not necessary to apprehend through sense-experience that to which a concept applies in order to know that it has application. All that is needed is that sense-experience should furnish good evidence from which the existence of an object falling under the concept can be safely inferred.

So it should not come as any surprise to hear that I think that I grasp the concepts of 'sight' and 'light' as completely as most sighted people in understanding that sight, like hearing, is a faculty of perception but one that is dependent on the functioning of eyes, that light is an object and facilitator of seeing as sound is of hearing, that looking is directed seeing as listening is directed hearing, that there are differences between glances and stares, glimpses and full views, loving looks and freezing looks, quizzical looks and solemn looks, that I have already a fair idea of what these differences are in detail, and that I believe that I could pretty quickly find out what I don't know about them if I wanted to. Nor again, since I already know through my tactile and kinaesthetic senses about the size and shape of objects, and about space and distance between objects, should it be surprising that I believe myself to understand judgements made by sighted people about such matters (even though, like most sighted people I suppose, I don't understand much about the mechanisms involved in making such judgements, and in particular find some difficulty in grasping how what must come to the eyes as two-dimensional presentations get turned into three-dimensional pictures). After all, there is generally a very good fit between the judgements I make about such matters on the basis of my own non-visual experience and the judgements made by sighted people on the basis of sight, except only that like many blind people I find that some estimates of distance made on the basis of sight are not very accurate. This not only confirms for me that I understand what they say about such matters but provides me with a basis in my own experience for considerable confidence in their sight-based testimony in general. Since objects can feel to me rough or smooth, strong or fragile, dirty or clean, new or worn, warm or cold, in motion or at rest, why should I not understand sighted people when they say that objects look to have some or other of these characteristics?

Colour words and visual aesthetic judgements might seem to be problematic for people who have no memory or experience of seeing, and I really do hope soon to be able to discuss these at some length. For the moment let me just say that I don't think that the main *concepts* involved are any great problem for people like me. After all, sounds too have what is called colour, due to the different harmonics of different instruments, colour which can be soft or hard, dark or bright (for blind as well as sighted people), mellow or garish. Paralleling the clashes and matches of visual colours, dissonances and consonances can be heard. But quite apart from that it is not difficult to grasp the idea that light of different frequencies might have different effects on those who see it, and that some of these effects, and some combinations of them, might be more enjoyable, cheering or soothing than others.

In fact, if you think that there are some visual concepts which people like me cannot grasp, or grasp fully, I have to ask you to say what they are, or what it is in them which must elude us. What is it that you can think about, which can play a role in the inferences you make, which we cannot think about, which cannot play a role in our inferences? Whatever the missing something is, if it cannot be articulated it cannot affect the validity of inferences, and is therefore not conceptual, at least as I understand concepts.

But of course if what you are talking about is not what I would call concepts but *words*, then I agree that there is something present in many vision-related words for many people which is not directly present in them for us, namely associated visual imagery, and more generally that part of their experiential meaning which relates directly to the experience or memory of seeing. Imagery and/or other aspects of experiential meaning are and must be irrelevant to conceptual meaning, but they are part of the total meaning of words to those for whom they have experiential meaning. Even colour words can still have some experiential meaning for people like me, as I shall explain more fully in a later letter; but that part of experiential meaning which consists of visual imagery, or which in any case relates directly to the experience of seeing, must always be missing from the experiential meaning of words for us. That fact does not diminish in the least, I believe, our ability to receive, or to communicate, knowledge or ideas about sight or its objects, or to participate in rational discussion about these subjects, or about anything else; but it is a fact, and it probably does diminish our chances of being good at certain kinds of rhetoric or poetry, or good in a certain way at rhetoric or poetry.

It should not be thought that the fact that vision-related words cannot have experiential meaning for us of a kind directly related to the experience of seeing means that we can have no kind of sympathetic understanding of the visual experiences of others, or of the experiential meaning of vision-related words for sighted people. If a sighted woman tells me that she is haunted by a visual image of the face of a dead child, either because of her own experience or because of a story she has read, that is intelligible to me not merely in the sense that I can understand the conceptual meaning of what she says but also in the sense that I can imagine something of what she is going through, and be moved by it. That could be because I can imagine what it would be like to be haunted by the sound of the voice of a dead child, but I don't think it needs to be that. One can be moved simply by thoughts. But I think there are two different degrees, perhaps amounting to two different kinds, of sympathetic understanding. There is the kind achieved as a result of the exercise of the imagination (a faculty whose exercise need not involve the presence to the mind of images of any kind, although it seems that it very often does), and there is the kind based on the actual remembering of an identical or closely similar experience of one's own (again: remembering, in my view, need not involve the presence of any imagery, although it often does). Some people have exceptionally strong imaginations, and can recreate for themselves (and for others too, if they are writers or actors) experiences of others which they have never themselves had. But even they probably do this better still if they have themselves had the same sort of experience. In any case, most people are able to identify much more strongly with those experiences of others which they remember themselves having, and that is another of the major advantages of having experience of one's own.

Blind people who do not remember ever seeing, though not necessarily without any sympathetic understanding of the visual experiences of sighted people, are therefore likely, nevertheless, to be deficient in this kind of understanding of such experiences, since they cannot bring to bear on it directly relevant experience and memories of their own; and of course they are unable to find in words any experiential meaning for themselves related to experience or memories of seeing. To that extent the experiential meaning of words with visual reference

111

is attenuated for them, and they are limited in their sympathetic understanding of the visual experience of others and in the vision-related content of the experiential meaning of words for sighted people.

That is, I think, the truth contained in the passages quoted from your letter early in this section of the present letter. But I still think that it is right to say that born-blind people can understand a very major part of the meaning of visual terms, not only because in an enormous number of their uses words have no significant amount of experiential meaning for anyone, and because some visual terms do have some experiential meaning for born-blind people on account of the similarities and overlaps between seeing and other modes of sensory awareness, but chiefly because conceptual meaning, which is wholly accessible to them, constitutes such a large part of the total meaning of words. Words enable us to do many things to others and to ourselves – to arouse and to quieten, to frighten and to comfort, to bully and to entreat, to berate and to encourage, to infuriate and to amuse, to torture and to delight, to quarrel and to agree; but they can do and mean all this and more only because they enable us to think and to convey thought. The conveying of conceptual meanings and of propositions picturing with more or less accuracy how objects corresponding to these meanings are related to one another is their chief role, and they can play that role for blind people just as much as for anyone else, since propositional pictures are not sensory images of any kind but thought-pictures.

III   Closing Remarks

I had hoped to discuss more fully in this letter not only colours and visual aesthetic questions in their relation to blind people but also the different ways in which blind and sighted people get to know a person. I also hope that we might soon be able to look at some differences in psychological make-up among blind people themselves, and indeed among sighted people. But again this letter is already long enough.

Before I close it, however, let me revert for a moment to a question raised in your last letter, to which I responded to some extent in my last letter but on which I would like to say another word. You wondered to what extent born-blind people miss sight. Because of the way our discussion has gone, and in particular because of my repeated emphasis on the abilities of people born blind, and of people like me, to understand what we might not be expected to understand, you may have got the impression – despite what I said about this in my last letter – that *I* at least don't miss sight very much, and don't think it very important. One thing that is true is that neither I nor, I think, most blind people who don't remember seeing miss the *pleasures* of sight very much. It is not that we don't believe that these pleasures are many and intense: I for my part wholly accept that for many sighted people the loss of the pleasures of sight are a major part of the total loss that blindness brings, and for some by far the most important part. But although, as I argued in my last letter, one can long for pleasures one has not experienced, I don't think that people born blind or without memory of seeing do pine for the pleasures of seeing flowers, sunsets, works of art, or even the faces of loved ones. Nevertheless, nothing in this or my previous letters is meant to imply that sight is anything other than a marvellous and precious faculty. The practical problems of being blind *are* serious and almost ever-present; but in addition, although I don't long for the pleasures that come through the eyes, and although I have argued, I fear at boring length, that blind people are not cut off

113

in principle from any kind of knowledge – I do constantly miss the amount of knowledge I would get, and the ease and rapidity with which I would get it, if I had sight. Also – and this is what I particularly wanted to emphasise at this point – I am repeatedly struck by how *interesting* it would be to see. I often think, as I sit in a bus or walk in the streets, not that it would always be pleasurable but that it would be endlessly more interesting to be able to look at people's faces. I say this not to arouse sympathy but only to try to counteract the impression which I fear both this and my previous letter may have tended to give of complacent self-satisfaction with my condition of blindness. I don't think I feel that. But it's just because we blind people do have real problems and deficiencies that it's particularly important not to have unreal ones attributed to us.

Yours ever,
Martin

Letter 6

FROM BRYAN MAGEE

TO MARTIN MILLIGAN

Dear Martin,

First let me make it clear that this letter is written in response to your Letter 4 only. Just as I finished writing it, and was reading it over, your Letter 5 arrived. My reply to that will have to constitute a separate letter, which will be number 7. When I have written that I shall send you both of them together.

Letter 4 provided me with not just food for thought but a banquet. I knew when I embarked on this correspondence that there would be golden fields to harvest but I underestimated their extent and also, I think, the problems involved in harvesting them.

Typical of the sort of question I raised in my opening letter was: 'What difference does the fact that you are blind and I am sighted make to the empirical concepts we form – for instance our conception of what it is to know a person?' Although it now makes me feel foolish to say so, I took it more or less for granted what the difference between being blind and being sighted was, and I expected us to need only a brief discussion of that before moving on to what I saw as the main question, namely what difference *that* difference makes to our respective conceptions of reality.

I now realize that this is not the case. What the difference is

115

between being blind and being sighted is a tricky question – or rather an umbrella under which cluster a dauntingly large number of tricky questions. As you rightly say on the second page of your Letter 4, we cannot avoid addressing ourselves to these before we go on to consider the implications of their answers for our respective conceptions of the world. This is going to compel us to discuss non-philosophical questions. But that is not something I think we need worry about. It has always seemed to me intellectually unserious to turn away from interesting questions on the ground that they do not wear the right label. In this correspondence I don't think we should worry ourselves about what is and what is not a philosophical question. 'What is a philosophical question?' is itself a philosophical question; and, what is more, it is one to which different philosophers have notoriously given incompatible answers. In any case we should usually expect to find philosophical problems embedded in a context of non-philosophical questions about the way things are.

A great deal of your letter seems to me to be motivated by a fierce conviction – no, something more driving than that, a ferocious determination – that blind people are not to be regarded as inferior because they are blind. The vividness and force of the feeling seems to be caused by the fact that this is how they are generally held in most of the world, and how they were generally held in Europe and North America until only recently; and that even in Europe and North America the desirable changes in attitude are far from complete. With all this I agree. And what is more I empathize with the emotions you feel about it. In my book *The New Radicalism*, published in 1962, I wrote, on page 59:

> What all human beings have in common by virtue of their common humanity is such that by comparison the differences are negligible.

However bestial some people may be, the fact that they are people is more important than the fact that they are bestial. And as for distinctions such as male and female, able and incompetent, rich and poor, educated and illiterate, Black and White, Communist and democrat – these pale into insignificance beside the fact that we are all people.

During the years immediately following the publication of that book I made many documentary programmes for television of which that passage was really the subtext – programmes about blacks, homosexuals, prostitutes and their clients, drug addicts, criminal psychopaths and all sorts of other human beings, including members of the Communist Party. In those days one had to put forward embattled arguments even for women being regarded as fully paid-up members of the human race. Giving full recognition to the common humanity of all of us, and then putting that recognition into practice in our social attitudes and arrangements, was an issue on which I can claim to have been, in a small way, something of a pioneer on television. Two documentaries I made about homosexuals – the research for which I then published as a book which was translated into many languages – were credited at the time with contributing something towards bringing about fundamental changes in the law. So I really do understand the feelings you have about the principle involved, and I share with you some of their intensity.

But the point, surely, is that human beings should be treated as of equal human worth, equal value, equal moral importance, and as having equal rights and opportunities, and being entitled to equal consideration. It is not that they are descriptively the same, or can do the same things, or that there are no important differences between the lives it is open to them to lead. The fact-value distinction makes itself felt here at its most insistent. Some individuals are capable of a great deal less than others in matters of enormous practical significance, and yet they are of equal worth *as human beings*. Those permanently paralysed from the neck down are in the cruelest sense of the word crippled, and life is full of things they cannot do, but *as people* they matter as much as anyone else. Some religions express this by saying that we are all equal in the sight of God, or that God loves us all equally. I am not religious, but I subscribe to the view of human beings that such phrases are trying to articulate. All people, whatever their capacities or incapacities, are to be fully respected as persons, and never, never patronized. At the same time it would be absurd, especially in extreme cases, to deny the factual, purely descriptive differences between them. Indeed, denial of such realities is likely to get in the way of dealing with them as they should be dealt with.

I think it essential that we should not muddle two different considerations here. There is a tremendous drive in your letter to play down the differences that exist in practice between the blind and the sighted, obviously because you do not want the blind to be held in lower esteem than the sighted. But this attitude could lead our whole enterprise astray. It is essential to our investigation that we should be truthful about what these differences are. In fact we have undertaken the task of putting them under a spotlight and examining them. This is in head-on collision with the view expressed in your letter that 'it is seriously wrong and harmful to lay great stress on those differences between human beings which cannot easily be removed or reduced', and unless you are willing, as I hope you are, to regard the conditions laid down in the remainder of the sentence in which those words of yours occur as having been fulfilled by the rest of your own letter, I don't see how we can go about doing what we have embarked on.

But that is not the only obstacle. Your anger has a personal edge. You suspect me personally of having written in a way designed to put the blind in their place, and on page 54 you remark snidely that I appear to have found your presumption exasperating. You suspect me of suspecting the blind of being unable to form intimate private relationships with the sighted, and fruitful working relationships with sighted colleagues, and to function satisfactorily in society at large – and therefore you suspect me of regarding them as people whose proper place would be outside society, confined to their own company. I in fact think none of these things, and what is more I said none of them. On the contrary, in the letter that launched this correspondence you will find that on pages 2–3 I either said or very clearly implied the opposite on each one of those counts.

What we should both be trying to do at this stage is identify and bring out clearly some of the crucial experiential differences between the sighted and the blind, as a preliminary to asking what further differences these in their turn make to our conception of the world. In doing this there will be no thought in either of our minds of anybody's being superior or inferior to anybody else. This has nothing to do with it. And do not suspect me of harbouring such thoughts unexpressed. When you spatter me with words like 'missionary', 'preaching' and 'gospel' in the last paragraph on page 60 you misconstrue my attitude as perversely as you did in attributing to me feelings of exasperation at your so-called presumption. The passages of mine to which you apply those words are written in terms which I am fairly sure most sighted people would assent to. I have to some extent tested this conjecture by trying the passages out on people, and always with the same result. I think you have gone wrong in not taking seriously what I actually wrote. I said that there was something foundational to *ordinary living* about seeing, and that in *ordinary living* our everyday moment-to-moment human interaction could not occur *as it does* if visual experience were not shared. The words I now place in italics are words I then used, and they are what I meant. And the statements in which they occur are true. The situation of the blind is not ordinary, and a great deal of the moment-to-moment human interaction that occurs between the sighted passes them by – as you movingly illustrate in what you say on pages 60–1. But from this fact, to which you agree, it never entered my mind to draw the false inference that blind people cannot communicate with others in a wide range of ways, including some of the most subtle, and relate to them on a wide variety of bases, including the most intimate, *by other means*. On the contrary, I know that they do, and it is this that gives rise to many of the questions we must address.

Our greatest difficulty is that a direct comparison of what it is like to be blind with what it is like to be sighted can be made only by someone who has been both, and neither you nor I are in that position, at least for practical purposes. But this is not an obstacle to our task. On the contrary, if you could remember seeing, your empirical concepts would have visual content, and these differences between us that we want to probe would not exist. So it is essential to our project that this difference should be there.

Diderot notes this in his *Letter on the Blind* – which I have just read, and in which I found much that you and I have already written in our own letters. 'We are curious,' he says, 'of seeing sight given to those who were born blind; but, on further consideration, philosophy, I believe, would be found a greater gainer by questioning a sensible blind man. We should learn the state of things in him, and could compare them with the state of things within ourselves; and perhaps we might from this comparison come at the solution of the difficulties which made the theory of vision and of the senses so intricate and so uncertain.' He also says: 'To prepare and question one born blind would not have been beneath the combined talents of Newton, Descartes, Locke and Leibniz', and I am now being made aware of the penetration of that remark.

Another book I have just been reading is *Touching the Rock*, by John M. Hull,[1] not about a blind man becoming sighted but about a sighted man becoming blind, which happened to the author in his forties. It is full of arresting contrasts between the two different worlds of experience. Here is just a handful of examples:

> It takes a blind person longer to get to know somebody. (p.16)

> The face no longer has the central place for me which it has in normal human relationships. (p.17)

> I am finding it more and more difficult to realize that people look like anything, to put any meaning into the idea that they have an appearance. (p.18)

> The blind person's perception of the world, sound apart, is confined to the reach of his body, and to any extension of his body which he can set up, such as a cane. (p.28)

> The tangible world sets up only as many points of reality as can be touched by my body, and this seems to be restricted to one problem at a time. I can explore the splinters on the park bench with the tip of my finger but I cannot, at the same time, concentrate upon exploring the pebbles with my big toe. I can use all ten fingers when I am exploring the shape of something but it is quite difficult to explore two objects simultaneously, one with each hand. (p.61)

> The intermittent nature of the acoustic world is one of its most

[1] Arrow Books edn., 1991.

121

striking features. In contrast, the [visually] perceived world is stable and continuous. (p.63)

For the deaf person, people have an abiding presence. They are there, all the time, every day. For the blind, people are not there unless they speak. Many times I have continued a conversation with a sighted friend, only to discover that he is not there. (p.72)

Sighted people find it difficult to realize that, for a blind person, the body itself has become the organ of sense. Apart from the white cane, and the sounds from the environment, the body's knowledge of its own surroundings does not exceed its own dimensions. This is such a curious position to be in, such a strange kind of reality for the body in the world, that the sighted can hardly grasp it. (p.119)

The different ways in which the blind person experiences motion indicate that the normal relationship between the body and the world has been severed. (p.136)

These are dramatic differences, and their implications extend beyond immediate thought. Yet they constitute only a few of the things Hull writes about. He has, for instance, a remarkable passage (p.102) about how different it is for the sighted and the blind to visit a new city, and how different are the terms in which they form their respective conceptions of it, so that the very name of it conjures up something quite different to each of them afterwards. Waking up in the morning is different (p.52): 'The important thing about waking up is not the morning but the presence. I am restored by wakefulness to the presence of the ones I love.' I have to say that Hull's description of these and a host of other differences between the blind and the sighted carry the ring of truth to me. I gather, moreover, that his book has been well received by the blind as well as by the sighted. Between those who have only ever had the sort of experiences listed on one side of these contrasts and those who have only ever had experiences on the other there must be immense differences in the nature and content of their empirical concepts, despite the fact that they are employing the same words for them – 'city', 'face', and the rest – and managing to communicate with one another by means of them: *must*, that is, if the widespread and long-held belief of most Western philosophers is correct that, to be truly significant, empirical concepts need to be derived from *and cashable back into* experience.

The fact that effective communication can take place between language users for whom the connotations of the concepts they are employing is so different is partly to be explained by the fact that the denotations remain the same. For both of them, 'London' means that particular city that is the capital of England; 'waking up' means ceasing to be asleep and becoming conscious; and the rest. This remains true independently of the deep differences in character between their experiences of being in London, of waking up, and so on. Even so, some awkward questions are raised about the cashability of empirical concepts back into experience. I am not in agreement with the later philosophy of Wittgenstein, but one of its attractions would be that it offers a possible way of answering such questions.

However, I am digressing – or perhaps just racing ahead too fast. I drew Hull's book into our discussion so that I could cite a blind writer who insists, in graphic terms, that the experience of the blind lacks irreplaceable qualities and content compared with that of the sighted, without being open to the suspicion of wanting to put blind people down, or patronize them, or regard them as incapable of living socially integrated lives. Having done that, I want to claim the same privilege for myself. I want to be able to say candidly what I think without having my motives questioned, most of all if I get it wrong. We must be honest about the differences of belief between us, and argue them out to the best of our ability. In other words we must *have* the argument, not shirk it. If you are prepared to go along with this, I shall have no regrets that so much of your last letter consists of a hot-blooded attack on views I did not express and do not hold. Impassioned statements of the need and right of blind people to be woven in amongst everybody else in the warp and woof of human society still need, alas, to be made, and yours included things that were new to me, so I learned from it. But I regarded it as a digression, at best a bonus. Let us now get back to the point.

There are some concessions that I must make to you. The heat you diagnosed as having entered my writing at one point was indeed there, though it had quite other causes from those you assumed. But I told you at the time what the chief one was: an anger at the way the emotional, sensory and aesthetic aspects of life tend to be persistently downgraded by otherwise intelligent people in favour of the intellectual aspect – which of course has its place, and an important place too, but still as one among others, and not the most important one. Interestingly, in just the same way as embattled emotions whose real sources lay outside our correspondence spilled over into your last letter, so did they into mine, and I admit that. Perhaps this should put both of us on our guard. In my case, whatever undertone of pugnacity crept in has its origins in a certain strand of my personal history.

I was trained in academic philosophy at Oxford during a time when linguistic philosophy was the reigning orthodoxy. I never subscribed to it, but because the fashion for it was so dominant I was usually in a minority of one when I criticized it, at least in any group of philosophers. One of my objections to it was its persistent tendency, because of its almost exclusive concern

with language, to proceed as if all knowledge were propositional knowledge. None of its adherents, so far as I know,
argued this openly, but much if not most of their philosophical
activity presupposed it. They talked as if Man were *homo loquax*.
My battles with individual followers of this fashion went on for
so many years, nearly always with me the odd man out, that the
subject became one on which I was liable to get heated. And – to
be honest – I did feel that you slid into the error in question near
the top of page 47 when you queried whether there was *in
principle* any knowledge to which the blind were denied access.
If the answer to that question even *could* be 'no' then it would
have to be possible for all knowledge to be, or to be adequately
translatable into, propositional knowledge; and I maintain, as I
always have maintained, that this is impossible. The same error
also, I thought, reared its head between the lines of what you
said about Rupert Cross. To me it seems plain that what Rupert
was saying was that he could form no adequate mental image of
what the nature of the Chairman's knowledge by acquaintance
was with Professor Brown's revelation of dissent. (One thinks
here of Hull's point about his losing his grip on the ability even
to attach any significance to the idea of someone's having an
appearance.) In every other way, of course, Rupert understood
perfectly well. I did not report him as being puzzled, though
you write as if I did. What I reported was his own explanation of
why he surmised that the sense most akin to sight was touch
rather than hearing, and why he therefore tended to think of
seeing as feeling-at-a-distance, so that it was via this analogy
that he arrived at his working conception of the sort of way in
which the Chairman was made aware of Professor Brown's
reaction. As for one of your other remarks about him, although
it is true that he would have had the sophisticated 'feel', as you
describe it, for any strange room, it is also true that he could not

have known the precise number, location, size and shape of all the physical objects in it without feeling them in a more literal sense, and could certainly not have taken them all in instantaneously on entering the room in the way a sighted person could.

Your description of some of the multifarious ways in which the blind can make up for their lack of sight is very instructive. On this point it may interest you that when I was a small child I had a vivid non-visual awareness of the nearness of material objects. I would walk confidently along a pitch black corridor in a strange house and stop dead a few inches short of a closed door, and then put out my hand to grope for the knob. If I woke up in the dark in a strange bedroom and wanted to get to a light-switch on the opposite side of the room I could usually circumnavigate the furniture in between, because I could 'feel' where the larger objects in the room were. I might knock small things over, but would almost invariably 'feel' the big ones. I say 'feel' because the sensation, which I can clearly recall, was as of a feeling-in-the-air with my whole bodily self. Your phrase 'atmosphere-thickening occupants of space' describes the apprehension exactly. I suddenly 'felt' a certain thickness in the air at a certain point relative to myself in the blackness surrounding me. The receptor sensation was not consciously experienced as being localized to my face, still less to my ears, though of course it may have been without my realizing it – as a small child I was not given to precise self-observation. And I lost this particular sense well before my teens. This illustrates your point that the blind develop potentialities that the sighted have also been endowed with but do not develop because they have less need of them. The same, I suppose, applies to memory, though of course that is not a sense. When I was a teenager I would emerge from a play or film with something close to a total recall of it that would stay with me for two or three days before fading. While it was with me I could supply almost any line of the dialogue on demand, and if what I had seen was a musical and I had enjoyed it I could sing all or most of the songs. But, again, I lost this ability in the course of growing up. You are right to surmise that I still retain some general sense, without the use of my eyes, of what sort of space I am in, and how densely or otherwise it is filled with material objects; but this has degenerated into something rough and ready, and is primitive now compared with what blind people develop. However, the most intriguing to me of all your observations in this vein is your surmise that blind people *think* more than sighted people. That is an unexpected observation, yet it seems obviously true when one reflects on it.

As far as I am concerned you successfully make the case that the gap between what the blind can do and what the sighted can do is nothing like so great or in the sighteds' favour as they suppose. You really have enlightened me about this. But having sincerely conceded this to you, I still think you push your case too far. It is, for instance, beyond the bounds of possibility that a blind person should play and win at snooker – a proposition which you do not assert but which obviously you take seriously. Playing the game at all involves being able to take in, in full detail, the situation created by up to twenty-two balls of varying colours occupying random positions on an oblong surface measuring twelve feet by more than six. This situation has to be perceived with exactitude, and the differences between the colours are of the essence of the game. To be in possession of a verbal description of it will not serve, because one has to achieve an integration of situational grasp with the application of physical skill. Snooker is entirely different in this respect from chess, where physical skill in moving the pieces has no place. It would be more like expecting a blind man to play spillikins. In any case, when the snooker table is full, a verbal description of the situation would take up to half an hour to formulate for each position, and could not be constructed without the use of reference points which a blind person would not be allowed to establish. According to the rules of the game it is a foul to touch any ball on the table by hand, or with any item of clothing, indeed other than by striking the white ball with the tip of one's wooden cue. In each shot one has to strike the white once only, and with such precision that it then travels a distance that may be anything up to thirteen feet and hits another ball at just the point on that other ball that will make the second ball move off in exactly the direction one wants it to, characteristically into a pocket at some further distance from the object ball and off to one side at an angle. A blind person, not able to see the balls and not allowed to touch any of them with any part of his body or his clothing cannot but be completely at a loss in this game.

So whichever blind person told you that he plays and wins at snooker is fantasizing. This suggests he is refusing to face the reality of his situation. And so are many other blind people you refer to in your letter, for instance the 'substantial number of intelligent and competent blind people in the USA who support the views repeatedly propounded by Tom Jernigan . . . to the effect that blindness is not a handicap but just a difference.' However, what really interests me most at bottom about all this, and what is philosophically most significant about it, is not anything about the blind at all; it is the fact that many if not most human beings do exactly the same thing, systematically but in another way, in that we construct a total conception of our situation out of the input we contingently have and then proceed as if what this leaves out cannot really make all that much difference – as if total reality cannot but correspond pretty well to the experience we have of it, and therefore anything we lack must be something we can compensate for fully, or almost fully, in other ways.

I am quite sure that in practice a large number of human beings believe that total reality consists of what they are capable of taking in, and that outside this there is nothing *and cannot be anything*. Most of the thinkers I have argued with who regard themselves as being in the empiricist tradition talk as if they believe this. Whenever one hears people say that this world is all there is, then *that*, or something very like it, must be what they are saying. Yet it appears to me to be almost certain that we are able to register a fraction only of what there is, and that we remain unable even to conceptualize most of the rest. When I tried to make this point in my last letter I intended it more radically than you took it, but that was my fault for expressing it in the way I did. You would be right to point out that in saying that we might imaginably have had bodies that were equipped to transmit, receive and interpret radar, television, radio, or X-rays I am giving clear expression to the thought that we lack senses we might have had, and that I am giving specific expression to what they could have been; and furthermore that I have some notion of what it would have been like to perceive objects in terms of them. So in those cases I have a pretty good idea of what it is that I lack. But the point I was groping my way towards, though I failed to get a firm hold on it, rests on the fact that I am able to give examples at all only by picking on entities of which I already have the concept, and which therefore derive from things that are already within the realm of human experience – and then, of course, you are able to say that I can conceptualize them. However, it is only since the discovery over the last two centuries of the various waves I instanced that it has been a possibility for anyone even to formulate my examples. In the perspective of history it is scarcely yesterday that these waves were discovered, and before that it was impossible for anyone even to think the thought that we might have been equipped with them. Not even the greatest geniuses of all time, such as Plato and Kant, were able to entertain the thought that we might have had, but happen not to have, bodies that are equipped to transmit and receive television. But the point I most wanted to make is not just that all human beings are perpetually in that situation with regard to all discoveries that are future to the time in which they happen to live their lives: I am saying that human beings *as such* are permanently in that situation with regard to everything that they will never be able to plug into their bodily apparatus (mental as well as sensory) either directly or via some intermediary device. And when you reflect what pathetic little creatures we are, and how limited and contingent the physical apparatus is through which everything we can apprehend has to be made available to us, it appears to me as certain as anything unprovable can be that we are passed completely by by most of what there is. In the nature of the case, if you say to me: 'What, for example?' or even just 'What *sort* of thing *might* it be?' I am at a loss to reply. There are no words. The concepts do not exist. Nor will they, ever.

It is here that purely rational reflection leads us to a point that must be either at the limits of reality or on the threshold of a transcendental metaphysics. Both are possibilities, but the former is the more unlikely one. As I said in Letter 3, it would be an astonishing coincidence if the limits of what we are able to apprehend with the particular apparatus we happen to have are also the limits of what there is. It is far more likely that a great deal lies permanently outside the limits of what it is possible for us to apprehend. And if that is so we shall never be able to

Jeames Thin

BOOKSELLERS est. 1848

EXCHANGE POLICY

We will gladly issue an exchange where the
following conditions have been met:

* The Customer has a valid till receipt
* The exchange must be requested within thirty days of purchase
* The returned goods must be in mint condition and unused
* The goods must be normal stock items

This does not affect your statutory rights

Jeames Thin

BOOKSELLERS est. 1848

EXCHANGE POLICY

James Thin LTD
57 George Street
Edinburgh
EH2 2JQ
VAT No 271 411 888

0753805030   1 @   6.99
Sight Unseen PB   £6.99

TOTAL PURCHASES: £6.99
PAYMENT: CASH   £7.00
CHANGE: £0.01
RECE   2824:101299:1338:01   Staff

Thank you for your custom

conceptualize it, think about it, talk about it, write about it, or in any way entertain notions about it, or communicate with one another about it. Yet it seems to me we are justified in asserting that its existence is considerably more probable than its non-existence. In case you think I am beginning to sound religious, let me assure you that I am not religious in any normal sense. There is no religious contraband I have hidden away, hoping to smuggle it into our discussion at some point. I am a non-religious person doing his best to argue rationally and to follow the argument wherever it may lead. At no point in this process, not even at the very end of it, does any act of faith come into the picture as far as I am concerned. Whatever total reality is, it is a plain, unvarnished, entirely non-magical fact that that is what it is; and what I am saying now is that it is virtually certain that most of it is unconceptualizable by us. This is a conclusion to which one is compelled by the ordinary processes of rational thought, it seems to me.

One of the many points you made that struck home was that the amount of a sighted person's environment that is sensorily available to him is nearly always pretty small. I think you meant when you said it that the proportion of what could or might be seen that is actually seen by any given person at any given moment is small. That of course is true. But to it I would add the argument I have just developed, namely the near-certainty that most of what there is lies outside the apprehension of nearly all of us permanently. If *that* is true, we are in the position of a group of people who live out the whole of our lives in the cellars of some castle without ever leaving the cellars or making contact with anyone else, and therefore never even knowing that the castle exists, still less that we are living in it. If we were to stumble across a transistor radio lying around somewhere and started playing about with it we would discover, no doubt to our bewilderment, that every point in the invisible air surrounding us was occupied simultaneously not only by a babble of voices talking different languages but by whole symphony orchestras, jazz bands and pop groups, all of which this little plastic box made instantly available to us. Yet even so, none of this would give us any inkling of the existence of the castle in which we were living.

What cannot be known cannot be known, and what cannot be talked about cannot be talked about. But I am constantly made aware that the sense of total reality possessed by someone who thinks along the lines I have just been outlining is radically different from that of someone who identifies the objects of possible experience with total reality. What constantly brings the difference home is the perpetually revealed presupposition on the part of so many people that the world of actual and possible experience is all there is – a presupposition for which I see no evidence whatever and which all the probabilities are against. It has never ceased to baffle me that so many people not only fail to see what these probabilities are but treat the opposite of what is probable as self-evident. It is like asserting that because all the sheep Kant ever saw were in Königsberg and its surrounding countryside he would have been justified by the Principle of Induction in inferring that all sheep were in Königsberg and its surrounding countryside. I had many reasons for embarking on this correspondence with you, but far and away the most important among them was the hope that I might gain new insight into the way in which my human equipment limits what I can apprehend. Every time you catch me insisting, conjecturing or assuming that the blind cannot apprehend this or that, there will always be at the back of my mind the question whether or not some parallel obtains with my own situation.

This thought leads me back to your conception of the sense you lack. If, you ask, I accept that all of us can attach meaning to certain words or groups of words that denote things that none of us has experienced, such as 'black holes', 'a building a hundred miles high' and so on, why can I not also accept that 'sight' is a concept which born-blind people could derive from or construct out of other non-visual concepts representing what they *have* experienced. My answer is that 'sight' differs from your other examples. Black holes are phenomena whose existence we infer from the theories of physics, above all Einstein's General Theory of Relativity. At the time of writing, their existence has not been empirically confirmed, and it might yet turn out that they do not exist. Meanwhile I understand the concept because I know enough physics to see how it comes about that the existence of such phenomena is to be expected on the basis of currently accepted theories. 'A building a hundred miles high' can be analysed into the concept of an empirical object which is thoroughly familiar to me in experience, namely a building, combined with two abstract notions which I know how to construct, namely the number 100 and the measurement 'a mile' – to which must be added the concept 'high', and that is one with which most of my spatio-temporal experience has directly familiarized me. In the same way all your examples can be analysed without remainder into constituents of two kinds – empirical concepts that I can relate to my experience, and abstract concepts whose provenance I understand – but such is not the case for the born-blind with the concept 'sight'. For them the very core, the heart, of the experience from which the concept is derived is inaccessible in experience. When you talk as you do of constructing the notion of sight out of non-visual concepts it is as if you were to talk of constructing the notion 'a building a hundred miles high' out of non-architectural and non-computational concepts.

Taking your actual conception of sight as it has been articulated thus far in our correspondence, one of the ingredients missing from it is the realization that seeing is an appetite, and what is more a greedy and lustful one. It is something the urge to satisfy which is almost irresistible for most of us for most of the time when we are up and awake. This was what I took, and still take, Aristotle to be referring to in the passage I quoted to you. When the University of Chicago translation[2] that I used has him say that 'we prefer seeing ... to everything else' I spontaneously took this to mean that in ordinary circumstances we prefer seeing to *doing* anything else. This seems to me the natural construction to put on his words, especially if you consider it, as I do, a true statement (unless one excepts being conscious and breathing). I am certain Aristotle did not mean that we would rather keep our sight than our loved ones. What he is referring to is this almost ungovernable lust to see that most of us have. During the day, provided always that we are awake and breathing – and not ill, sunbathing or dozing – the very first thing that most of us want to be doing is seeing, and we are seriously disturbed if we cannot do so, even for a brief time. In fact it induces a sort of panic in most people. Even by ordinary act of will, to keep one's eyes closed is extraordinarily difficult for long. A common way of maltreating prisoners in today's world is to put bags over their heads or to keep them blindfolded for long periods. You may remember that some years ago the British Government was condemned at the European Court for sanctioning this in Northern Ireland. Many prisoners in such circumstances get into a distressed state and become disoriented, some start hallucinating, some have nervous or even psychotic breakdowns – and all because they

[2]Richard McKeon, *Introduction to Aristotle* (rev. ed., 1973).

are prevented from seeing. By the sighted, seeing is felt as a *need*. And it is the feeding of this almost ungovernable craving that constitutes the ongoing pleasure of sight. It is as if we were desperately hungry all the time, in such a way that only if we were eating all the time could we be content – so we eat all the time.

Because this realization seems to be lacking, your conception of the pleasures of sight appears altogether too aesthetic, as if someone were to suppose that the only pleasures involved in eating and drinking were those of the gourmet. There are, of course, aesthetic visual pleasures, but for most of us these are associated with rare or special occasions – looking at a painting or a landscape, seeing a beautiful woman, going to the ballet. Not many of us are lucky enough to see beautiful objects every day, whereas the normal pleasure of seeing, which is some sort of hungered-for and deeply needed satisfyingness, accompanies us all the time we are awake. Hence Aristotle's remark. I remember reading somewhere that seeing consumes about a third of our total energy, and it would not surprise me at all if this were true.

You, however, write as if there were two reasons only why one might want to see: for its practical usefulness and as a source of aesthetic pleasure. You even go so far as to surmise that the second of these might not weigh much with you personally on account of your puritan disposition. For what it is worth, aesthetic visual pleasure as such is not of a kind that present-day puritans disapprove of – at least, I have never heard any of them do so. It is an exceptionally pure kind of aesthetic pleasure, perhaps the purest of all. When people object morally to visual art it is usually for one of three other kinds of reason; first religious – for instance because our official religion forbids us to make graven images; second, the treatment of the subject matter – for instance because an object of religious, political, or social veneration has been presented sacrilegiously, or a sexual act disturbingly, or violence brutally, or a nauseating object realistically; or third, because the artist has flouted the expectations of the spectator to such a degree that the latter feels outraged, for instance that he is having his intelligence insulted by being served up with nonsense and invited to take it seriously.

The practical usefulness of seeing plus its power to provide aesthetic pleasure come nowhere near to accounting for the awed value that sighted people place on it. There are several other large ingredients. One of course is the sheer avidity of the desire to see which I have just now tried to describe. This has no parallel with the senses of hearing, taste or smell: we are under no slavish compulsion to be hearing sounds all the time, or tasting tastes, or smelling smells. However, there might be a similarity with the fifth remaining sense, that of touch. If we could obtain no sense of physical contact with anything at all, even for quite a short time, I suspect we might find that psychologically disturbing too. The experience of weightlessness is said to be disorienting. The word 'orientation' may perhaps provide us with a clue here, for sight is the chief means by which sighted people consciously orientate themselves from moment to moment in their ordinary world. This huge and immediate dependence that the sighted have on sight brings me to another ingredient. You say of sighted people on page 56 that 'the sense of which they make overwhelmingly the greatest use is sight'. If all the significant content of empirical concepts is ultimately derived from sensory experience (a view you say you share) does this not mean that 'overwhelmingly' more of the content of our stock of empirical concepts is derived from sight than from any other sense? I think it does. And I rate this as borne out by personal experience and observation: it seems to me that most people's conception of things, of the world, of reality, including other people, is so heavily weighted with vision-derived content that if that were removed what was left would seem to them so drastically impoverished as to be scarcely any longer a world. This is borne out by John Hull in *Touching the Rock* (p. 153) when he writes: 'Sighted people live in the world. The blind person lives in consciousness.' He is here overlooking the fact that visual experience is as much 'in consciousness' as any other sort of experience, but his words corroborate my surmise that most sighted people's conception of the world is predominantly vision-related.

In fact I would even go so far as to say that there is an unreflecting tendency in sighted people to assume for a good deal of the time that the way things look is the way they actually are, thus conflating visual representations and reality itself. I have recently had an example of this in reference to you. When I reported to someone that you felt no urgent drive to be able to see, and that you believed you could get to know another human being as well as sighted people could, my companion said: 'But surely he must long to know how people really are?' I do not think this use of words is justified, but I also do not think it is uncommon. Since you sharpened my vigilance I have noticed over and again that when people discuss the possibility of the blind regaining their sight they say things like: 'It must be amazing to realize after such a long time how things actually are.' This assumption that things *are* their visual appearances, or at the very least that what they are *'really* like' is their visual appearances, seems to me to permeate the whole of our language. The assumption is that what you see with your eyes is *it*, the thing itself, the real thing, which otherwise you are not fully in contact with.

Perhaps this is the moment to make the point that the primal human error of epistemological realism – the illusion that we have direct access to physical objects, that we are in immediate contact with them – is facilitated and may even be caused by our contingent possession of this particular sense of sight. To quote John Hull's book again, he writes on page 63: 'The world of being, the silent, still world where things simply are, that does not exist [for the blind]. The rockery, the pavilion, the skyline of high-rise flats, the flagpoles over the cricket ground, none of this is really there . . . The acoustic world is one in which things pass in and out of existence. This happens with such surprising rapidity. There seems to be no intermediate zone of approach. There is a sudden cry from the lake, 'Hello Daddy!'; my children are there in their paddle boat. Previously, a moment ago, they were not there.' And in the same vein (p. 42): 'Other people's voices come from nowhere . . . The disappearance of the face is only the most poignant example of the dematerialization of the whole body. People become mere sounds. This leads to something else. Just because there is nothing to mediate between the intangible sounds of voices and the immediate contact of bodies, body-contact becomes all the more startling. A handshake or an embrace becomes a shock, because the body comes out of nowhere into sudden reality.' The quotation, 'Many times I have continued a conversation with a sighted friend, only to discover that he is not there,' which I cited earlier from page 72, continues: 'He may have walked away without telling me. He may have nodded or smiled, thinking the conversation was over. From my point of view, he has suddenly vanished.'

Such formulations as these make me feel that some sort of Kantian ontology – an ontology of things as they are in themselves existing not just independently of our experience of them but independently of the *modes* in which we experience them – might have commended itself to us quite naturally, and without any of the difficulty it seems to present for most people, were it not for the exceptionally delusory nature of this particular sense of sight that we happen to be equipped with. Visual experience, as I have remarked, is every bit as much an occupant of conscious awareness as all other kinds of experience, and is in our heads just as the others are; but this is not how it feels. Uniquely (except perhaps, again, for the sense of touch) the experiences themselves seem to be 'out there', not 'in here'. For this reason too it is extraordinarily difficult, if not sometimes impossible, for us to detach our notion of a material object from its visual appearance. If we possessed only our sense of hearing we would probably find it impossible to believe that the objects of our perception are not in themselves sounds, that in themselves they are something categorially different from sounds. But given that we do in fact have our other senses this mistake is not a temptation for us. Yet exactly the same point with regard to our sense of sight – that material objects are not their appearances, and are in themselves categorially different from their appearances – is almost impossibly difficult to grasp, so much so that most people, it seems to me, do not grasp it, but reject it, in spite of the fact that it must be true; unless, of course, reality is Berkeleian, and nothing but appearances exists.

The most heartwarming aspect of your Letter 4 is its demonstration of the astonishing extent to which the deprivation of sight can be overcome by developing other resources and bringing them into play. As you rightly complain, most sighted people do not realize this, unless and until they are challenged to do it themselves, or watch someone close to them doing it. One consequence of this, in the light of what I have been saying, is that they are inclined to take it for granted that if they were to lose their sight they would be partially cut off not only from the external world but from the richest single source of the content of their inner lives. John Hull went through a terrible period after he had become completely blind in which he thought this had happened to him. 'Being invisible to others I become invisible to myself. This means that I lack self-knowledge, I become unconscious. This is what the archetype of blindness indicates, the loss of consciousness, the descent into sleep, the sense of nothingness, of becoming nothing' (pp. 45-46). 'I feel as if I have become nothing, unable to act as a father, impotent, unable to survey, to admire, or to exercise jurisdiction or discrimination. I have a strange feeling of being dead' (p. 47). 'It no longer matters where I am. I am dissolving' (p. 48).

Ordinary language is full of expressions which indicate that ordinary people tend to think of eyesight as the touchstone of what is precious: phrases like 'precious as sight' or 'as dear as sight' are in everyday use. Also in everday use is the word 'blind' to mean 'unaware' or 'impervious' – 'he is blind to x' means 'he is unaware of x' or 'he is impervious to x', and this use of the word is a good deal commoner than the literal one of being without sight, because sighted people have more occasion to employ it that way. Of course, a normally sensitive person would tend not to use expressions like this within the earshot of the blind, who may therefore not realize how common they are. But they occur also throughout our literature. Only the other evening I saw *King Lear*, and in the first few minutes of the play came that wonderful speech of Goneril's protesting her love for her father:

> I love you more than word can wield the matter;
> Dearer than eyesight, space and liberty;
> Beyond what can be valued rich or rare;
> No less than life, with grace, health, beauty, honour;
> As much as child e'er loved, or father found;
> A love that makes breath poor and speech unable;
> Beyond all manner of so much I love you.

It is surely of some significance that none of our other senses are talked of in anything like this way, neither in ordinary speech nor in literature generally. People have a unique attitude to eyesight in this regard.

Since embarking on this correspondence I have seized on every opportunity that has come my way to talk to blind people and raise our questions with some of them. The most recent said to me that when people lose their sight it is common for them to grieve as for the death of a loved one. He went on to surmise that the emotions involved in these experiences of bereavement and mourning were not just vaguely comparable but essentially the same. For reasons derived from everything I have said so far in this letter I do not believe that the explanation you offer for this is the right one when you say near the middle of page 57 that 'large numbers of recently-blind people are disproportionately depressed or damaged in spirit as a result of the widespread acceptance of this exaggeration [of the importance of sight, and therefore of its absence].' For you write as if the recently blind were responding to a prevalent but mistaken social attitude, whereas it seems to me that they are responding spontaneously to direct experience. Interestingly, this is another and yet different example of your attributing to what can be expressed in propositions and their verbalizable presuppositions something that I believe is to be understood only in terms of direct, non-verbal and not-fully-verbalizable experience. The recently blind know what they have lost. You do not. They know *and love* what they have lost. Of its kind it was uniquely precious to them, they crave its return, they cannot imagine getting through the remainder of their lives without it. None of this seems to me disproportionate, and certainly none but a trivial amount of it due to what other people may harmfully say or think. On the contrary, it seems clear to me that the mourning is proportionate to the loss, and that this is why it occurs. What can be said on your side of the matter, I believe, is that for all but a minority the process of mourning, whether for the loss of a loved one or the loss of sight, works itself out over a period of time, after which people come to terms with their loss and enter on a new phase of life in which they are able to experience happiness once more in the absence of what they had previously considered indispensable. (No doubt in many there is a part of the psyche that never does get over it – I could truthfully say that there is a part of me that has never got over the death of my father, but this in no way prevents me from living a normal life, and I may go for days or even weeks at a time without thinking about him.) This, I would suggest, is the phase in which all the things you have to say about blindness not being the permanent cataclysm it is commonly supposed to be make their validity felt. But I suspect that the phase of mourning has to be gone through first, and cannot be foreshortened, partly because it is a natural reaction and partly because it is itself a necessary purgative element in the long-term process of readjustment.

In further qualification, allowance has to be made for the fact that, as you point out, sighted people differ among themselves quite widely in the extent to which they are vision-oriented. But even the least such rely primarily on it for many of the fundamental daily necessities like moving about and recognizing others. You say that the philosopher friend who told you he didn't think he'd notice much if he went blind was almost certainly exaggerating. I would say he was deceiving himself. Nor do I consider it a coincidence that he was an academic. In our society, at least, a good many people who are untypical enough to relate to the world and others less through their senses and emotions than through ideas are to be found in academe. Their need, or failure, to respond with greater sensitivity to the world around them has for centuries been one of the stock themes of fiction and drama, whether comedic or serious. In any case, I am not sure that the severity of a handicap is accurately to be measured by the extent to which the people who have it think about it. The urge to adapt goes deep and is astonishing in what it can accomplish. I am always amazed, for instance, that so few of the prisoners in Nazi extermination camps had nervous breakdowns. If being in Auschwitz does not give someone a nervous breakdown, what would? If I were to lose a leg in an accident I'm sure I would learn after a while to do most of the things I do now, and to laugh freely again and enjoy life, and to spend little time thinking about my loss; and it might even be that coping with the initial trauma would strengthen my character and healthily rectify my sense of proportion; and it is certain that I would learn to do many things in new ways, and would develop capacities I had left underdeveloped before; but none of this would be to say that it would not be a terrible thing that had happened to me, or that I was not handicapped. Similarly with the point you make about the become-blind developing not only all sorts of sensory and physical powers that they had left uncultivated before but also developing new strengths of character, mind and spirit: I am sure that it is true, but I am also sure that such people would rather not have had the experience.

Since before Freud it has been central to our understanding of the psychology of individuals that the crucial significance of certain experiences may well not be reflected in consciousness. In fact, people may have no recollection at all of experiences that have had a decisive influence on their development. This, by the way, causes me a certain misgiving about classifying you with the born-blind. For you say on the first page of your Letter 2 that you saw 'perfectly well' for the first eighteen months of

143

your life. Eighteen months is a long time. It is claimed for many of the things we experience during our first eighteen months that they may have a lifelong effect on us even if we neither remember the experience nor possess any conscious awareness of there being a cause-and-effect relationship. If this can be true of other things it surely *might* be true of something as basic as seeing – especially in view of the fact that it constituted not just a single one-off experience but something you were doing all the time you were awake for a year and a half. However, as you imply, it is difficult, if not impossible, to know what allowance, if any, we should make for this. That being the case, I am prepared to follow you in going along with the classification of you as 'born-blind' for purposes of our correspondence, for the reasons you give, and because any other classification would be open to an equal questioning – though most of all because distinctions of that particular kind may have a limited relevance to the issues we find ourselves raising. But I do want to register a temporary unease with you, just in case it does turn out to matter.

Before the digression constituted by my last paragraph I was taking an insistent line about the unique specialness of sight to the sighted; but I do not want to hammer on about that, for if I did I would begin to give the impression of insinuating unjust imputations against you. On page 49 of your letter you say with simple directness that 'blindness is a major handicap and deprivation', so nothing I have said must be taken as implying that you deny it. If this statement of yours is held in mind throughout your eloquent exposition of the range and com-plexity of the countervailing considerations that have to be taken into account then perhaps something like a proper balance will have been struck. However, there is one point over which you swing the pendulum further in what might have been my own mistaken direction than I did myself, and that is when you say in the middle of page 50 that blindness is, or at least often is, a deformity. That thought had never occurred to me, and now that it does I do not accept it. But this is not something we need argue about. For myself, I suspect that the revulsion against blindness to which you refer on page 66 is based on a fear which in its turn is based on empathy. I am a squeamish person, and if I see anyone suffering from what I regard as a deformity I turn away with a violent uprush of revulsion. This is not directly a rejection of the person – though indirectly, alas, it has the same side-effects, and I am aware and ashamed of that. What is happening is that involuntarily, and hyper-vividly, I put myself in that person's position and am filled with horror at the thought of being in his situation. Desperately I try to get such a thought out of my mind, but of course I cannot do this while looking at him, so I turn away. From these experiences I would hazard a fairly confident guess that the revulsion of some people against blindness is similar: those who react in that way are overwhelmed with terror at the thought of themselves being blind, and are turning violently away from what imposes that thought on them, namely blind people. The explanation I would offer of *why* they are so terrified is implicit in what I have written earlier in this letter.

Finally, you make some good hits against me which I cannot do other than concede. For instance you are right to say how implausible it is to maintain that none of the virgins who long for sexual experience can have any idea of what it is they are missing. Mind you, a lot of powerful biological pre-programming is at work here – but then so it is in other areas of our life too, including, I believe, the acquisition of a language, and also our *a priori* disposition to perceive so-called external reality in the form of physical objects in a space and a time. But if you don't agree with these things let's not argue about them unless we have to.

I am also much struck by what you say to the effect that if the

145

blind were in the overwhelming majority, and controlled the world, and were able to arrange everything for their own convenience, they would still be handicapped and yet might not know it even though there remained a minority of sighted people. You and the H. G. Wells story have enabled me to achieve an insight about this which I found not easy to grasp, and which I doubt whether most sighted people have grasped.

With these last few remarks I think I have made all the comments I wish to make on your Letter 4. It would be silly for either of us to bang away at every little point in the hope of reaching agreement about it: that aim is unachievable, and our correspondence would become inexpressibly tedious if we attempted it. There is going to have to come a time in each exchange when differences are left to stand. It will be up to us to judge when that time has been reached.

My present hope is that we can now leave behind us most of the non-philosophical issues raised in your Letter 4. You stake out so much common ground in that letter – for instance the two main paragraphs on page 46, the two main paragraphs on pages 46–7, the new paragraph on page 48, the two paragraphs beginning on page 49, and striking phrases throughout such as 'born-blind people in our actual sight-dominated world' – and there is so much in all this that gives rise to important questions for us to discuss that I hope we can go on and discuss them without getting bogged down in other issues which hold out less promise of progress. In the final paragraph of your letter you express yourself impatient to move on to Letter 5 and 'some of the big philosophical issues'. I await that letter with eagerness.

Yours ever,
Bryan

Letter 7

FROM BRYAN MAGEE

TO MARTIN MILLIGAN

Dear Martin

I wrote my last letter, Letter 6, in response to your Letter 4 before receiving your Letter 5. This exploded over my head like a grenade. I had just been playfully teasing you with mock-accusations of the not-truly-believable crime of holding that all knowledge is propositional when all the time this is what you *did* hold. And now here it is, militantly expressed in your new letter. The words stand before me, or rather shout up at me from their context on page 84: 'All knowledge *in the ordinary sense of the word* is propositional'.

The experiences I had at Oxford and referred to in my last letter lead me to believe that if you and I try to resolve this difference before proceeding any further we may never get any further, and therefore never reach the questions which it was our intention to confront. Obviously whether or not all knowledge is propositional has a bearing on the question of what difference being blind or sighted makes to our conception of the world, and that indeed is why we have got ourselves into this present position. The trouble is that the question itself is one that can be discussed without any reference to the blind/sighted distinction. In fact, as far as my knowledge goes, that is how all philosophers until us have discussed it, except for their use of examples that might just as easily have been picked from other senses.

Quite apart from any past experience of mine, you know as well as I do that professional philosophy is a permanent battlefield in which contestants endlessly dispute the significance of terms such as 'meaning' and 'knowledge'. So, again, if you and I were to settle on a programme of coming to agreement on these and other such basic terms before confronting issues arising out of blindness we would never reach our main questions.

I want if I can to shift our discussion so that its specific focus is the blind/sighted distinction, and the differences which that makes to our conception of the world. But I don't want to evade the issues raised in your letter, especially after you've gone to all the trouble of formulating them. So I'll proceed in the following way. In this present letter I'll give my answers to your latest arguments; but I shall end by challenging you with some questions, and I hope your answers to these will put us back on track. Up to now the subtext of our correspondence has consisted to a large extent of my saying: 'Surely blind people must conceptualize this, that and the other in a radically different way from sighted people, and not be able to conceptualize certain things at all?' and your replying: 'Not a bit. We may not be able to do everything you can do but we can know everything you can know and are therefore full members of that community that is created by the forms of human intercommunication.' And this got us into a dispute about the nature of 'know'. But I fear it means we began by getting assertion and challenge the wrong way round for our purposes, because this way courts the perpetual denial of difference when the differences are what we set out to discuss; so I shall extend our subtext later by saying to you, in effect: 'All right then, what do *you* think are the main differences in the way you and I conceptualize *x*, *y* and *z*? Surely you are not seriously suggesting that we have the *same* conception of, say, space – or of a person? And if not, how would you venture a formulation of what the differences are likely to be?' Then, however much we may disagree, our exchange can become a discussion of differences instead of alternate assertion and denial that they exist. Anyway, let's try it.

Now, turning specifically to your letter. First with regard to the distinction between 'knowing' and 'knowing that' or 'knowing about'. That we can talk about the world, and communicate with one another about it in language, is one of the many miracles that most of us take for granted. Yet miraculous it remains. For thousands of years some of the most intelligent people have concluded that it is the possession of language more than any other single thing that differentiates human beings from animals. That is still a widely held view, and there is a passage in your letter that suggests that perhaps you share it. As you know, in the early years of this century Bertrand Russell did pioneering work on the question of how it is possible for us to talk about the world, a question which subsumes the question of how it is possible for language to be meaningful, which in turn raises the question of how it is possible for false statements to be meaningful, especially if nothing exists to which they refer. There are aspects of these problems on which Russell changed his mind, but one argument to which he held consistently was that if everything we could say were fully explicable in terms of other things we could say then the entire system of language would be circular. At no point would it be earthed to anything non-linguistic. Therefore this cannot be the case. It has to be that some elements of what is said are understood not in terms of other things that are said but in terms of something non-linguistic, for if that were not so there would be no point at which language made contact with reality (whether this be 'the world' or 'experience'). Throughout his changing logical analyses of the meaningfulness of language, therefore, he clung to the necessity for some distinction of this sort between what in our linguistic utterances can be understood in terms of other linguistic utterances and what is intelligible only in terms of non-linguistic experience.

Having gone with the argument thus far our next question becomes: 'All right, then, so what are the points at which our language plugs in to something non-linguistic?' It is essential to realize that this question arises only at the second stage – essential because if someone gives an invalid answer to it this does not invalidate the distinction that has given rise to it but means only that he has chosen the wrong candidate for a position that still needs to be filled. Russell himself changed his views about it. When he came to write *Our Knowledge of the External World*, which was published in 1914 (*The Problems of Philosophy* had been published in 1912), his candidate was sense data. There have been good philosophers since who were persuaded by this – for instance A. J. Ayer remained so until the end of his life.[1] But others found it implausible, many of them holding that we had direct experience of persons and objects. This led to what became known as 'The Basis Problem', the problem of what it is with which we are in direct contact, on the basis of which we build up our highly complex and largely abstract conception of the world. It was one of the problems that most divided the Logical Positivists. Indeed it is one of the fundamental problems of philosophy, especially for anyone who claims to be an empiricist, as you do. (My position

[1] Bryan Magee, *The Great Philosophers* 315.

embraces empiricism in the way Kant's did – I am an empirical realist, as were both Kant and Schopenhauer; but, like them, I also believe that some sort of transcendental idealism is inescapable. But in the present context this is enough to give me the same problem as I am insisting you have.)

Although in current philosophical discussion it is usual to attribute to Bertrand Russell the distinction between 'knowing' and 'knowing that' (as he put it in some of his writings before *The Problems of Philosophy*) there is at least one philosopher before him who asserted it as insistently as he did, and that was Schopenhauer. I do not think Russell had read Schopenhauer or was aware of the fact, but Schopenhauer places enormous weight on the distinction. 'I wanted in this way to stress and demonstrate the great difference, indeed opposition, between knowledge of perceptions and abstract, or reflected, knowledge. Hitherto this difference has received too little attention, and its establishment is a fundamental feature of my philosophy; for many phenomena of our mental life can be explained only from this difference.' He also writes: '*Perception* is not only the *source* of all knowledge, but is itself knowledge *par excellence*; it alone is the unconditionally true genuine knowledge, fully worthy of the name. For it alone imparts *insight* proper; it alone is actually assimilated by man, passes into his inner nature, and can quite justifiably be called *his* . . .'

The general view within which Schopenhauer incorporated this doctrine went something like this. Everything that exists is uniquely particular. That includes not only material objects but perceptions, thoughts and experiences. If we tried to find a separate word for each one, language would be not only unmanageable but unintelligible, because, for instance, I would be unable to understand any noun unless I knew already to what unique particular it referred. If language is to perform the

151

functions it does it has for the most part to pick out general features of things, and omit what is uniquely particular. From these general features we construct concepts that can be stored, communicated, and employed in innumerable and invaluable ways. But the concepts will have empirical content, that is to say will be 'about the world', only insofar as they are genuinely derived from experience – which is why Schopenhauer says that perception is the source of all knowledge. But this leaves us with a problem, which he expresses in the words: 'Concepts always remain universal, and so do not reach down to the particular; yet it is precisely the particular that has to be dealt with in life.' There is a great deal about the uniquely specific that simply cannot be expressed or communicated in words. Everyone has perceptions, feelings, moods, dreams and all sorts of other experiences that he cannot put into words. This problem, in Schopenhauer's view, is partially solved in every society known to us, however primitive that society may be, by art. It is the function, or one of the functions, of works of art to store and articulate unique perceptions, insights and experiences. However, it is in the nature of the case that one cannot say what these are, for that would be to give expression in words to what cannot be expressed in words. A piece of music that moves us conveys something to us, is meaningful to us, expresses something that may matter to us profoundly, yet what that something is is inherently inexpressible in language. The composer Mendelssohn showed an independent understanding of this when he wrote in a letter to a friend: 'The thoughts that are expressed to me by music that I love are not too indefinite to be put into words, but, on the contrary, too definite.' What any work of art expresses is expressible solely and uniquely by that work. This is true even of works that are themselves in the medium of language. It is impossible to say satisfactorily what

Hamlet is 'about' or 'means', or what *King Lear* is 'about' or 'means'. If someone asks us what a particular lyric poem means we cannot give him an adequate answer, for it is something that only the poem itself expresses. The composer Sibelius once played a recording of one of his works to a visitor: at the end the visitor asked: 'What does it *mean*?' whereupon Sibelius, without saying another word, put the record on again.

Partly on the basis of this distinction Schopenhauer developed a philosophy of art that was deeply insightful. Mahler, for instance (according to his leading biographer Henry-Louis de la Grange) 'thought that Schopenhauer's book contained the most profound analysis of music that had ever been made.' Correlative with Schopenhauer's distinction between, on the one hand, significance that can be stated and, on the other hand, significance that can be presented but not stated, is a distinction between, on the one hand, knowledge that can be put into words and, on the other, knowledge that can be acquired but not put into words. As a professional philosopher you will know that this was taken from Schopenhauer by Wittgenstein and made one of the central themes of his early philosophy as presented to us in the *Tractatus Logico-Philosophicus*. From that source it was taken up by Susanne K. Langer and redeveloped into a theory of art that took account (as Schopenhauer had self-evidently not been able to do) of early twentieth-century advances in logic. On the basis of it she drew one distinction in particular that I find illuminating, a distinction between what she calls discursive symbols and presentational symbols. Language, arithmetical numbers, musical notation and so on are all discursive symbolisms which, when they express content in use, have to do so in a relevant sequence: each symbol has to be spoken or written, heard or read, after the one before it and before the one after it, thus making their ordering in time or space an indispensable component of their meaningful use, such that if the ordering is changed the meaning itself may well be changed. On the other hand a work of art taken as a whole constitutes a presentational symbol, and conveys something that has to be grasped all at once as an organic unity, a *Gestalt* as you might say, and expresses a kind of significance that is exhibited only by the work itself; and this cannot be translated out into any equivalent that could be expressed in the sequential characters of a discursive symbolism. This kind of significance is the significance of art, and is exhibited but not stated. It is a form of meaning that can be shown but not said. I mention these developments not because I want to associate myself with every jot and tittle of them – still less would I deny that each of the writers I have mentioned was importantly wrong in some respects – but because I believe they are on the right track. They have got hold of the right end of the stick. And it is some such approach as this that informs my own attitudes.

I do not, by the way, think of concepts as words. Not only do I think all the things about them that you say, I also think that presentational symbols, which by definition are inexpressible in words, may legitimately be regarded as concepts – in fact it is perfectly normal to talk about a composer's or a painter's 'ideas', and legitimately so. Nor do I think of propositions as sentences, though I do (as you clearly do too) think of them as always expressible in some discursive symbolism – which I would remind you need not be language: it could be mathematics, for instance, or symbolic logic. Not all discursive symbolisms can express propositions – much musical notation, for instance, cannot, though some can. I dwell on words in the way I do because it is you who are maintaining that nothing can count as knowledge unless it is expressible in words, which must mean that when you talk of propositional knowledge you mean by 'propositional' – at least in this context – something that can be put into words.

I think your contention that all knowledge in the ordinary sense of the word is propositional, and is knowledge of truths, can be demonstrated in the following way to be mistaken. If you say to me: 'Do you know E. J. Moeran's Symphony in G minor?' I would truthfully answer Yes, and we would both be using language in the normal way. But my knowledge of Moeran's symphony does not consist in any knowledge of propositions or of truths (though it may *entail* knowing some propositions and truths – I shall come to that later). The work is a little-known[2] one, which is why I have chosen it as my example, for it so happens that most music-lovers would have to answer No to your question. Now there is no number of propositions, however great, that I could voice to such people that would put them in the position, in which I happen to be, of knowing the symphony. I could tell them all sorts of things about it: not just things extraneous to the work, like when it was composed, but things intrinsic to it, such as what instruments it is scored for, how many movements there are, how each one is structured and how long it lasts, what the key relationships within the work are, and so on and so forth. What I could not do is tell them the symphony. If I lectured them for an hour, at the end of that time those of them who were attentive and had retentive memories would possess a lot of detailed knowledge about the symphony, but to the question: 'Do you now know Moeran's symphony?' they would still have to answer No. If you then turned to me and said: 'What is it you know that they still don't?' the natural answer for me to give would be: 'Why, the

---

[2] Another normal use of the term.

symphony, of course. I know the symphony, and none of them does.' Knowing the symphony is not a matter of knowing propositions or of knowing truths, and yet it is unquestionably a matter of knowing something.

If I were to ask the person who runs the Salzburg Festival: 'Which of the conductors you engage knows the Mahler symphonies best?' he would answer, 'Mr X'. Now although a number of conductors are what you might call intellectuals, many are not, including some of the greatest; and Mr X might give the greatest performances in the world of the Mahler symphonies without being able to say anything of the slightest interest about them. He might well know nothing like as much about them as many a scholar, critic, or even well-read music lover, but he must be said to know and understand the symphonies as well as, if not better than, anyone.

You cannot claim that in either of my examples I have used the word 'know' in an unusual way. Would you, then, maintain either that Mr X can not really be said to know the Mahler symphonies, or that his knowledge of them is propositional? I do not see how you can do either. His knowledge of the Mahler symphonies is not a knowledge of truths, and this refutes your statement that 'a "knowing" which has been isolated from all knowledge of truths is not a knowing of any thing but a "perfectly and completely" empty "knowing" – a non-knowing.' In fact your letter teems with assertions that are refuted by my examples. For instance: 'I think that it is quite right that we should demand of anything which is to be granted the status of knowledge that it should be expressible in verbal language.' And 'perception, experiential knowledge ... is always propositional in form.' All such statements are refuted by our experience of the arts and by our knowledge of the arts: the experience of a work of art cannot be put into words, and nor can the knowledge of it – at least, not all of that knowledge, and not the most important part of it.

You tweak Russell by the nose for saying 'it would be rash to assume that human beings ever, in fact, have acquaintance with things without at the same time knowing some truth about them,' but your whole letter illustrates the prudence of his remark. For you make a good fist at showing that whenever we have direct knowledge of something we also know something about it. I could know Moeran's symphony without ever having heard or read a word about it, but to justify saying that I knew it I would have to know (except for the sort of momentary forgetting that can happen with the name of a well-known friend) how many movements it had. If I could not, even on settled reflection, produce that piece of information about the work I could scarcely be said to know it at all well. One often says to a publicly acknowledged expert on a particular com-poser: 'Do you know such-and-such a [virtually never per-formed] work?' and he says either No or something like: 'Well, I did hear it once, but I can't really be said to know it.' Such a person will commonly know pretty well everything *about* such a work that there is to be known: it's just that he doesn't know the work itself, or know it very well.

In my view, your mistake is in moving from the fact, if it is a fact (as Russell surmised), that every time we know something we also know something about it, to the assertion that all possible knowledge of it is comprised in what can be known about it. When you are challenged by a person who says: 'No, I am talking simply about the direct knowledge of it, not any knowing about or knowing that,' you are always able to point to whatever examples of 'knowing about' or 'knowing that' are inseparably associated with this particular bit of knowing, and then say, 'Look, you can't get away from this. Your claim to know X means you know that *p* and you know that *q*. If you don't know that *p* and that *q* you can't be said to know X.' That's true, he can't – like me with the number of movements in the Moeran symphony – but the two kinds of knowledge are not the same piece of knowledge, as I have shown. In argument one needs constantly to be on one's guard against slipping from the fact that one thing is inseparable from another into treating them as if they were the same. One cannot have colour without extension, but colour and extension are categorially different. You yourself have knowledge of extension by direct experience, but you can never have knowledge of colour by direct experience.

Your contention that the only significant difference between 'knowledge' and 'knowledge that' consists in how the knowledge is acquired by a given individual would have the effect of making it a non-difference as far as logic and analysis are concerned – indeed, I suspect as far as philosophy in general is concerned. It would become merely a difference in someone's biography.

Quite independently of everything I have said so far, your clinging to a position of: 'I would find it difficult to see how anything could be called knowledge ... if it couldn't be put into words' would land you into an insoluble problem with regard to the higher animals. You write: 'I would be very unhappy about saying either that non-language-using animals can't know anything, or that their knowledge was totally different in kind from propositional knowledge.' What, then, was their situation during those aeons before the evolutionary emergence of mankind, when there had never been any such thing as language and was not to be for millions of years to come? Did the higher animals then know things in terms of some ghostly proto-symbolism that bore no relation to any symbolism that had ever actually existed but derived significance nevertheless from the fact that the possibility of a more developed symbolism of a not unrelated kind was going to be actualized in a different sort of animal ages after their death? I do not believe you can believe it. But if what you want to insist is: 'They did know things, and what they knew was not unrelated to the sorts of things that are expressible in language,' you are conceding that knowledge can exist without language. And of course the subsequent development of language, like all history, was contingent, and need not have happened at all. If you want to say that their knowing things depended on the *possibility* of language even although that possibility had never been, and need never actually have been, realized, you are adopting a position that is metaphysical in a way reminiscent of the most scholastic medieval philosophers – and quite out of keeping with your general outlook, I should have thought – and, more to the point, one which I do not believe can be defended.

It seems to me as plain as can be that the higher animals have knowledge by direct experience. If one concedes this, and concedes also the categorial difference between this and knowledge by description, or propositional knowledge, no problem is presented by the fact that animals have knowledge but do not have language.

The notion that there are things that we can *really* know only if we have direct experience of them – something akin to Schopenhauer's view that direct experience is knowledge *par excellence* – is actually, I should say, common, and expresses itself frequently in ordinary language. I am thinking not only of extreme experiences, such as falling in love, though those may be what leap first to mind. Almost every day one hears people say things like, 'He doesn't know what fear is,' and 'She doesn't know what friendship is,' when what they mean is that the person in question has never had the experience in question and therefore, *for that reason*, does not really understand the phenomenon. Of decisive significance for the dispute between you and me is the fact that equally common variants on this are expressions like 'Fear? He doesn't know the meaning of the word,' and 'She doesn't know what the word "friendship" means'. The implication always is that to know what these things are you need to have experienced them yourself, and the person in question hasn't. Of course, in the Oxford-philosophy-speak that you and I are so familiar with you could say that the individual in question understands perfectly well what the word means whenever he or she comes across it in a sentence, and often makes appropriate use of it in sentences of his own, and never misuses it. But these are irritatingly trivial truths that fail to engage with the point.

In art and story, which are full of truths that philosophy misses, what I am saying is a common theme. One of the most famous of medieval legends is about a young man who sets out to learn what fear is. Various people try to explain it to him, and illustrate what they say in imaginative ways, but only when he finally experiences fear does he know what it is. Over and again in plays and novels and films we come across exemplifications of the idea that however much you may think you know something, when you actually come to experience it you realize that you hadn't known it at all. I could cite many examples, but one will be enough to drive the point home, a favourite moment of mine which occurs at the climax of Bernard Shaw's play *Saint Joan* and makes a colossal impact in live performance. The burning of Joan of Arc occurs off-stage, and everyone troops away to watch it, leaving the Earl of Warwick alone on-stage: he knows what executions are like and would rather not witness another one, particularly of a young girl. There is a long, deathly silence, during which tension in the audience mounts, and which is then broken off-stage by the terrible howling and sobbing of a man's voice. On to the stage reels a Chaplain from the English army who throughout the play has sincerely argued that the burning of Joan would, on certain conditions, be the religious, right and proper thing to do. As the stage direction describes it; 'The Chaplain staggers in from the courtyard like a demented creature, his face streaming with tears, making the piteous sounds that Warwick has heard. He stumbles to the prisoner's stool, and throws himself upon it with heartrending sobs.' Part of the exchange that follows is:

> THE CHAPLAIN. I meant no harm. I did not know what it would be like.
>
> WARWICK [hardening]. Oh! You saw it, then?
>
> THE CHAPLAIN. I did not know what I was doing. I am a hotheaded fool. And I shall be damned to all eternity for it.
>
> WARWICK. Nonsense! Very distressing, no doubt; but it was not your doing.
>
> THE CHAPLAIN [lamentably]. I let them do it. If I had known I would have torn her from their hands. You don't know: you haven't seen: it is so easy to talk when you don't know. You madden yourself with words: you damn yourself because it feels grand to throw oil on the flaming hell of your own temper. But when it is brought home to you; when you see the thing you have done; when it is blinding your eyes, stifling your nostrils, tearing your heart, then — then —

Not only is this terrific theatre, it also, like so much terrific theatre, displays profound truth about the way things are.

This view that there are many respects (no one says all) in which no amount of knowledge by description can give you the equivalent of knowledge by direct experience – a view that expresses itself so frequently both in ordinary speech and in the arts – is true across a wide field of application, and often down to the separate components of our experience. You cannot know what the taste of flesh is unless you have experienced it. You cannot know what the colour green is unless you have experienced it. And it will not do to say that we need to be in possession of a language to acquire such knowledge – the case of the higher animals refutes that. It may be that in all such circumstances language has the ability to shorten our journey by helping us on parts of the way, but never by itself can it take us to our destination.

Let me give an instance of the sort of thing I have in mind here about the relationship that usually obtains between experience and descriptions of it. I know from experience that I have an unremarkable palate, not coarse as you claim your wife says yours is, but not sensitive either. When once, long ago, I took a ten-day tasting course organized by Guinness I was told at the end that my results were average. On the first day I was confronted by a row of ten carburetors, each containing Guinness, and was asked to sample, and comment on, each one in turn. Most of them tasted pretty much the same to me, one or two a little different. The course organizer then explained to me that this one had been kept beyond the optimum life-span of the yeast, that one had been stored at too high a temperature, and so on and so forth. He then encouraged me to taste them again now that I knew something about them, and then again, and to go on tasting them until I no longer felt I was making any progress. Next day when I came in I was confronted by the same carburetors in a different order. But already each sample tasted different to me, and I could identify some though not all of the differences. As the course proceeded, the differences between the samples were gently reduced, new kinds of sample were introduced – and, to cut a long story short, at the end of ten days I was pronouncing not only that this one was too old but approximately *how* old, and not only that that one had been stored at too high a temperature but at approximately *what* temperature – and getting it right most of the time. Now it is perfectly true that I could not have reached this point without the perpetual explanations of the course organizer. But it is equally true that I could never have reached it either without perpetually repeated tastings of the Guinness – not even if the organizer had gone on explaining to me for ten years instead of ten days. Direct experience of tastes, and of minute differences between tastes, repeated over and over again, was indispensable to the acquisition of this knowledge – and there can be no question but that it was *knowledge* I was acquiring. Scarcely any of the subtle differences in taste that I had learned to identify and explain would have been expressible in words alone to someone who had not experienced them on his tongue.

Our human lives, so much wider and more many sided than that of animals, are replete with knowledge that cannot be acquired without direct experience. When I say that you cannot know France if you have never been there, however much you may have read and heard about it, or that you cannot know Brahms's Third Symphony if you have never listened to it, I am touching only the tiniest tip of an iceberg. You say you don't see how a 'knowledge by experience' could be exchanged. You are right. It cannot. There is no way I could impart to someone who never tasted Guinness the knowledge I gained on that tasting course. Mr X cannot tell someone else how to conduct the Mahler symphonies. I once had a long discussion with a successful middle-aged business man about the communicability of the knowledge of business he had acquired by

experience. My question was: 'Could you in principle communicate to a brilliant but inexperienced young man all that you
have learned, in such a way that he could then go out and do it
while he is still young? If not, why not?' After a lot of analysis
we came to the conclusion that the answer had to be that he
could not, though why he could not left us mystified once we
had got beyond a few rather obvious but partial and incomplete
explanatory points. I cannot give to someone who has never
tasted asparagus my knowledge of how asparagus tastes. I
cannot give to someone who has never seen anything yellow
my knowledge of what the colour yellow is. And yet again you
cannot say I am using the term 'knowledge' in anything other
than a familiar sense. As Schopenhauer put it laconically: 'If
perceptions were communicable, there would be a communication worth the trouble.' When David Armstrong said, as you
quote him as saying, that perception 'floods us with knowledge', he did not mean that it floods us with propositions.

In the course of making these points I have referred to, among
others, Schopenhauer, the early Wittgenstein, Susanne K.
Langer, and Bertrand Russell. Whatever our differences may be
in this correspondence, let them not be differences about the
interpretation of philosophers. That is not our concern here. We
don't want to get ourselves sidetracked into an argument over
what Russell or any of the others really meant, any more than,
as you rightly said at an earlier stage, we wanted to get
ourselves sidetracked into an argument over what Aristotle
meant. Something said by Gilbert Ryle a quarter of a century
ago resonates in my inward ear as a warning:

> When I was a young undergraduate philosopher and a young don
> philosopher, the intellectual atmosphere at Oxford was very
> stuffy. Most of my elder colleagues were so obsessed with writing

articles or giving lectures on the great and glorious dead that one couldn't start, or anyhow maintain, a discussion about anything without the subject being changed before long to 'Which dialogue did Plato say that in and did he really mean it?' and 'Could the Greek be interpreted in another way?' and so on . . . I'm not at all hostile to philosophical scholarship. Indeed, for good or ill, I've made lots and lots of my own shots at it elsewhere. But mixing the drinks is always a bad thing. In *The Concept of Mind* I wanted to raise and discuss an issue without side issues cropping up as to whether Kant had or had not improved on Hume in this or that respect, or whether Duns Scotus had been more original than Ockham on this or that point, or whether the text of so and so should have read in this way or in that way. Nice enough questions, but not ones that I wanted to discuss.[3]

I do not say we should never refer to other philosophers. Doing so is too useful to be abjured. If a well-known figure has established a distinction that you or I want to make use of it will usually be more sensible to refer to him or her than go to all the trouble of trying to remake the distinction before using it; and if the other one of us wants to say 'Ah, but that isn't really the distinction he was making', we can surely let it go at that, without haring off after the digression. You have given me the impression sometimes of perhaps wanting to engage me in argument about Russell; but I want us to keep our eyes on, and shoot our arrows at, our own targets. In the first full paragraph of your Letter 5 on page 78 you state in your own words, accurately and without reference to other writers, what my position is. The formulation is yours, and I give it my endorsement, so you can refer us back to it if and when the need arises.

[3] Bryan Magee, *Modern British Philosophy* 110.

But I hope we shall move forward in our coming letters and not keep going back over old ground.

In order to tie the ends up as far as this point, I want to make one or two brief and unconnected comments on matters in your last letter that I have not yet touched on.

Contrary to the consensual view among contemporary philosophers I agree with you that it is possible to be consciously aware without being consciously aware *of* anything. (That makes two of us, at least.) Like, I suspect, you, I have actually experienced such states, which is why I feel confident in bucking the consensus. The issue would be an important one if the question were whether or not a self exists that is independent of experience. But I do not see that as a question that is bound to arise in our correspondence. If it does, we may find that we agree about it.

Turning to something quite different, you have misunderstood me over the example of the gramophone record. The point is not the difference between the reproduction of recorded sound and the sound of a live performance. The point is the difference between a little disc of plastic and Beethoven's Choral Symphony. If 150 years ago you had handed someone a small shiny disc with a hole in the middle and said to him: 'This is Beethoven's Choral Symphony' he would not have had the remotest idea what you could possibly be talking about. If you had then said to him: 'A performance of the symphony is inscribed on this disc, in the grooves you see here, in such a way that if you put the disc on a machine designed for the purpose, and do certain things to it, the machine will give forth music that will sound to you indistinguishable (or nearly indistinguishable) from a live performance of Beethoven's Choral Symphony given by an orchestra of a hundred players and a choir even larger,' it would have seemed to him, if he believed you and had any imagination, like magic. My point was that there are good arguments for believing that if our representations are 'like' reality they are like it in the same sort of way as certain little plastic discs are like Beethoven's Choral Symphony, and for the same sort of reason, namely that they are recordings of it inscribed in an almost unimaginably different medium. When you say that the mystery of the correspondence between our representations and reality is no greater than that of the correspondence between a photograph and what it portrays, or a map and the terrain it charts, you take no account of the view that each of these last two examples is a case of correspondence between two sets of appearances, whereas the first would have to be a correspondence, if it is a case of correspondence at all, between something that is appearance and something that is not appearance. It is the possibility and nature of *that* sort of correspondence that I described as 'deeply mysterious'.

Not unrelated to this, I believe you also misunderstand the tool metaphor as used for the relationship between representation and reality, and that you do so partially by assimilating it to the picture metaphor. According to the tool metaphor our representations are not like reality in any sense whatsoever – any more than a thermometer is like a body of air whose temperature it tells us. What they are like is a set of readings on gauges that we have evolved in the course of our biological evolution as parts of our survival kit, monitoring our environment and informing us of changes in it that might affect us. The writer I know who argues this case most intriguingly is Hans Vaihinger in his book *The Philosophy of 'As If'*. It is his view that the most fundamental mistake we make in our conception of the world is that we mis-take the readings on our gauges for pictures of what they measure. In other words he argued in epistemology something parallel to what the later Wittgenstein was to argue in terms of our use of language – and I do indeed believe that Wittgenstein owed Vaihinger an unacknowledged debt. But Vaihinger's work is altogether more direct and profound. (As Russell did, I see the early work of Wittgenstein as being work of genius, and I think we still have something to learn from it despite what are now its obvious defects; but, again like Russell, I think his later work is misguided and tends to lead astray those infected by it. Vaihinger, by contrast, is a much under-valued figure in the English-speaking world.)

A different point. When I said that it would be logically impossible for all knowledge to be propositional knowledge, one thing I had in mind was Russell's argument that if this were the case the entire system of language would be circular, and would have no necessary connection at any point with non-linguistic reality. His argument on this matter seems to me watertight and fundamental. It is perfectly true that some people have embraced its implications at their most radical and said: 'Yes indeed, he is right: there is no non-linguistic reality to which language refers. Every book, scientific theory and articulated piece of language whatsoever – plus unarticulated verbal thought – is a structure of words *within* which we may seek for coherence and meaning, but to which nothing outside itself corresponds.' Far more people take that line in literary theory than in philosophy, I suspect because philosophers are more aware of the difficulties involved in defending it. By applying our scientific theories through technology we build bridges that stay up under heavy loads, airplanes that actually fly and carry millions of people where they want to go, rockets that journey to outer space: every day innumerable events testify to the fact that there is a non-linguistic reality that must correspond pretty closely and in many respects to what we say and believe about it. The idea that language is a self-contained system is a non-starter for anyone not divorced from reality. You are right to say that concepts and propositions can stand in *logical* relationships only to other concepts and propositions, but – quite apart from the fact that there are many other sorts of relationship besides logical relationships – my position does not breach that principle. For, as I have shown, we have knowledge by direct experience, and we know that we do, and therefore the proposition that we have knowledge by direct experience is true; and this truth is incompatible with the circularity of language.

Since I know you do not hold the view that there is no non-linguistic reality to which language refers I have no need to argue against it in our correspondence. Both of us believe that human utterance is in some way 'about' the world, or that it can be, and often is. Problems posed by this 'aboutness' have provided the subject-matter for some of the most interesting and influential philosophy to have been produced in the twentieth century. Since the only possible logical validation of a proposition must itself be propositional, such validation cannot be provided by non-propositional direct experience. Yet most philosophers, including all empirical philosophers (though not those alone, by any means), want to cling to the idea that our knowledge of the world, even if it is not derived from experience, can ultimately be validated only by experience. It means that any such validation could not be logical. So they have the following serious problem: if an experience cannot provide logical justification for a statement, how, if at all, can it provide justification for the truth of any statement? To my mind the most fruitful approach to this problem is the one opened up by Karl Popper in his book *The Logic of Scientific Discovery* – not his well-known doctrine of falsifiability, since the logical falsity of a statement can be derived only from other statements, but his treatment of the problem of the empirical basis, and of basic statements. He rejects justificationism altogether. But since this is not an issue between us I do not need to go into it here.

The use of language relates in some essential way to a non-linguistic reality at both ends, not only the 'object' end but also the 'subject' end. And both are problematic – not only the relationship of language to the world but also the relationship of language to the intentions of language-users. This too has been the subject of much interesting philosophy in the twentieth century. However, what we are concerned with here is what might be called the putting into language of experience which is not in itself linguistic, and I am not sure that this is a philosophical problem. It is an empirical question, it seems to me, and as such one for brain scientists, perhaps experimental psychologists, not for people whose equipment is merely philosophical. But perhaps you do not agree with that. I should be interested to know.

Talking of empirical questions, I was told the other day by an eye surgeon who is much involved in research into the physiology of seeing, and is a leading figure in this field at Oxford University, that between twenty and twenty-five per cent of the cerebral cortex is devoted to seeing, and that there is no other activity to which anything like so much of the brain is given over – certainly not the use of language. Since being told this I have read something by Oliver Sacks which claims that the proportion is closer to half. In either case it has fascinating implications. What is cause and what is effect may be difficult to disentangle, but that so much of the brain is devoted to sight would appear to connect with the fact that the conception of the world that sighted people have is so overwhelmingly dominated by vision-related content, to the extent that they customarily confuse visual sensory data with an independently existing reality in external space. It also brings home how great the difference is likely to be between such a conception of the world and that possessed by born-blind people. One surprising result of research in only the last ten years (the eye surgeon told me) is the discovery of how refined the division of labour is among cells in the eye, and how particularized the connection is between these and cells in the brain: there is an individual cell in the eye that deals with a particular colour, and a one-to-one connection between this and a single cell at the back of the brain that processes the information from the eye. In the case of people born blind these pathways are never joined up, and those parts of the brain never activated, at least not for seeing. What happens to them, he says, is that they become available for other uses. I asked him what would be the case with someone like you, who saw for eighteen months and then had his eyes removed. He replied that a whole elaborate network of neural connections between your eyes and your brain would have been formed, and the development of a large part of your brain would have been activated for purposes of seeing: however, he said, as soon as your eyes were removed these physical connections would have begun to deteriorate with disuse, and at the age you were then the brain is still so malleable that it could well be that all traces of your early visual development eventually disappeared, and that those parts of your brain became adapted to other uses. This is a process that he would expect to occur to differing degrees in different people, and therefore he would not make confident pronouncements about an individual he had not investigated. He did say, however, that your view that you are now in the same condition as the born blind could well be correct not only as regards your subjective psychology but also as regards your physiology, the actual condition of your brain.

He asked me, as almost everyone with whom I have discussed this correspondence has asked me, whether I have questioned you about your dreams. It surprises me that this point occurs so quickly to nearly everybody other than myself: it suggests a difference between me and them. But anyhow, the reason for the question is obvious to me. Although, clearly, I can't assert that this is true of everyone, it appears that the dreams of sighted people are not only predominantly visual, often exclusively so, but commonly of a degree of vividness that is never experienced in waking life, and could not be experienced in waking life (except under the influence of a psychedelic drug). What is more, this aspect of dreaming is the salient one for most dreamers: when it comes to dreams, 'vivid' seems to be the adjective more characteristically used than any other. This otherwise-never-available intensity of visual experience has enormous impact on the dreamer, and he responds to it with a corresponding intensity. It is what he most remembers when he wakes up. It is so sharply engraved on his mind that it will often haunt him for days afterwards. Indeed, there are some dreams that constitute such powerful experiences that one remembers them for the rest of one's life. Now, presumably, none of this can be true for you in visual terms. People are curious to know, then, if it is true for you in any terms. They want to know how you dream.

If I were to essay a paraphrase in aural terms of the experience the sighted have when dreaming, it might go something like this. Not realizing that you are asleep and dreaming, you find yourself in a world that consists of nothing but sounds. These sounds are unnaturally bright and alive, so much so as to ravish your attention. They have a glory and richness that no words could describe. If the sound is of people speaking, their voices are like celestial clarinets, and each syllable is of such an exquisite beauty regarded sheerly as sound, regardless of its meaning, that it pierces you to the heart like a music more beautiful than any you have ever heard or could imagine. If it is a bird singing, every note falls into the space of your dream like a droplet of ambrosial nectar. Even nothing more than the sound of a rushing wind sets all the leaves glittering in the valley of your mind. Every sound of whatever kind is ecstasy in the ear, gorgeous and wonderful, deep-toned and substantial, satisfying in some utterly fundamental and unnameable way. So firmly does the experience seize possession of you that you are taken over by it and become one with it. You *are* what you hear. It is all so real that when you wake up you are astonished to find that it was 'only a dream' – and disappointed to find that you do not exist in such a world after all but in one where the ringing of your alarm clock does not sound like Heifetz playing the violin, and the car horns outside the window are not the trumpets of the Apocalypse.

It is because dreams are some sort of visual equivalent of this that they are endlessly referred to in ordinary speech as the touchstone of wonderfulness, the actually experienced incursion of magic into everyday life; and they play this role throughout the arts and popular entertainment, from the most severely classical and ancient to the latest pop lyric. Human beings from the most primitive times till now have regarded dreams as having an exceedingly special significance in life, though their interpretation of what that significance is has gone through many changes.

I have looked up dreams and dreaming in the index of T. J. Carroll's excellent and (I understand) classic handbook *Blindness: what it is, what it does, and how to live with it,* only to discover that there are no entries. Do you have dreams whose experiential impact is of a vividness unparalleled in waking life, in the sort of

173

way I have tried to indicate, though for you in terms other than visual ones? If you do, can you say anything about them? And do you know anything about the extent to which you are typical? Is there any lore about dreams among the blind, any handful of notable and generally accepted truths? Many beside myself would be fascinated to hear.

But let me come, in the end, to some of the specific questions we embarked on this correspondence to confront. Let us take the concept of a person. When I question people about this their answers seem to depend very much on whether or not they are religious. These days, of course, most people are not, at least not in any very serious sense. They seem to associate a person exclusively with his body. Even so, most of them seem to make some sort of distinction that is not unlike that in computers between hardware and software. The piece of hardware that is the body has had all sorts of software programmed into it by way of upbringing, experiences, education, skills, memories, and so on, and these are now stored inside it and available for use; but there can be no question of their being able to exist by themselves, independently of the body. People who take this sort of view seem to think of each combination of hardware and software as a unique human being. But in spite of their recognition of the importance of the software they usually say, if pressed, that they find it impossible to conceive of any of this without the computer itself, the body, and that perhaps for this reason the concept they form of anyone they know consists predominantly of a visual image of his body, more particularly his face, with which they then associate whichever of the invisible attributes stored within are appropriate to the context in which the person is being thought about. The visual image is always the core entity to which those other associations are attached. If pressed harder to try to think of the person without any visual associations at all their first reaction is nearly always to conjure up the sound of his voice, usually on the telephone (because this is when they are accustomed to hear him without seeing him) – though this, apparently, evokes almost immediately, and involuntarily, a visual image of the person again.

The religious people I have spoken to see the matter differently. Although their religious views vary widely, they seem to be at one in believing that each of us has some sort of essential self that is not physical, and is associated only temporarily with our body, and not only could exist independently of the body but one day will. Many of them say that, because this essential self has no perceptible attributes, when it comes to the people they know they have difficulty in forming any actual conception of it that does not make 'as if' use of one of their perceptible attributes as a prop. Most commonly that seems to take the form of a bloodless, thin-air version of an image of the person's visual appearance, the sort of way the dead are commonly represented in stories and in films (no doubt that is *why* they are so represented), that is to say a translucent visual image of the person that floats effortlessly about in space, into and out of, and through, physical objects. In other words, although they think they know, or they believe, that the essential Bryan Magee is something separate from his visual appearance they will still find themselves using a pallid and insubstantial version of their customary image of that appearance as a focus or substitute for something they would not otherwise be able to hold in mind.

What a contrast all this is with John Hull's experience after he had been blind for only a few years! On page 18 of *Touching the Rock* he writes: 'Increasingly, I am no longer even trying to imagine what people look like. My knowledge of you is based upon what we have been through together, not on what you look like. There is a further development. Not only do I not know or care what you look like (although I still have a few qualms and doubts in the case of women), I am beginning to lose the category itself. I am finding it more and more difficult to realize that people look like anything, to put any meaning into the idea that they have an appearance.'

Now I presume that you do not possess the category of 'visual appearance' at all for practical daily purposes, that is to say for your actual working conception of the people you know. What is a person to you?

From what I know of you I would not expect you to hold religious beliefs, yet there must be many blind people who do. Would you expect their conception of a person to differ categorially from yours? If so, how might the difference be articulated in words?

At the risk of raising too many questions at once I want to ask about one more concept, namely space. I do so partly because you raise it yourself in your last letter and I do not want to let it pass without response, and partly because I want to give you a choice of questions to reply to. If you want to keep us to one question at a time hereafter, please do: if you wish to hold this particular question on standby there is no difficulty about that. But in any case you say that you and other blind people are struck by how often judgements of distance that are based on sight are inaccurate. You do not expand on this, and it would be interesting to hear you do so. I would like you to go further and dilate on your concept of space in general, and the ways in which experience has taught you that it differs from that possessed by sighted people. Hull emphasizes the transformation in his working conception of space that was brought about by blindness. There is no reason why you should agree with Hull, and in any case your experience of blindness is different from his, but sooner or later I shall be fascinated to hear your views on the subject.

And now, I think, the time has come for me to finish this letter. We have, both of us, allowed our wagon trains to fan out far too wide, and it is in the interests of both of us not to let them spread any wider, but to draw together the impedimenta of our discussion into something closer to a linear formation in which everything can be seen to be heading in the same direction. Above all, we ought to keep the blind/sighted distinction at the centre of our discussions and not get ourselves into arguments that can just as well be conducted without reference to it. I hope you agree with that. If you do, I shall be happy to follow whatever path you choose.

Yours ever,
Bryan

FROM MARTIN MILLIGAN
TO BRYAN MAGEE

Dear Bryan,

Many thanks for Letters 6 and 7, which you sent me together. It was thoughtful of you to hold back Letter 6, in which, though also saying some nice things, you were maybe a bit hard on me in parts, until you could send the more serene and calming Letter 7. I enjoyed all of the later and almost all of the earlier letter very much, and I think both have helped to carry forward our discussion.

One of the things I was very glad of in Letter 6 was that you there brought John Hull's book *Touching the Rock* very fully into our discussion. As you know, it had not yet been published, and neither of us knew anything about it, when we exchanged our first letters. I had still not been able to read it when I wrote Letters 4 and 5. But it is not only an exceptionally well-written and interesting book about one man's response to blindness: it is one which contains much of direct relevance to the issues we are concerned with. Your many representative and telling quotations from it help to highlight issues on which we have to focus. I propose to comment quite a bit on Hull's book in this letter, in part because although it has been quite widely read, I think, by blind as well as by sighted people, and received sympathetic treatments on more than one broadcast, it has not as far as I know been much discussed or written about by blind people, at least in Britain – certainly not as much as it deserves. My chief reason for giving quite a lot of attention to this book is that I want to respond to your indications that you would like me to be more specific about how my experiences as a blind person differ from those of sighted people, and what other differences these differences make, and because responding to some of the things Hull says will help me do that.

I do very much agree with you that at this point in our discussions we ought to try to move forward and not spend too much time going back over old ground, so I won't pause too long now to try to explain at all completely where I think you have got me wrong in your Letters 6 and 7. But two misunderstandings I must try to clear up before going any further.

I Segregationism and Visionism

The first is revealed in the sentence in Letter 6 in which you say 'You suspect me of suspecting the blind of being unable to form intimate private relationships with the sighted, and fruitful working relationships with sighted colleagues, and to function satisfactorily in society at large – and therefore you suspect me of regarding them as people whose proper place would be outside society, confined to their own company.' Elsewhere you imply that I accused you of being in effect what I call a visionist.

In fact I have never entertained or expressed any such suspicions about you. When writing Letter 4 I did not know the full extent of your splendid work in the humanist cause in the 'sixties', but I did know something of the humane and liberating character of your book on homosexuals published then. I did remember the passages in your very first letter, to which you refer in rebutting my alleged suspicions, and above all I knew from the contacts we have had that you are an enlightened and humane person quite free of patronisingness or even embarrassment in your relations with blind people. That is in part why I was surprised, and expressed surprise, that you should say without qualification that the differences between blind and sighted people 'can only be described as vast', that to those capable of it seeing is preferable 'to everything else', that 'there is something foundational to ordinary living about visual experience', and that 'everyday moment-to-moment human interaction is predicated on the fact that this experience is shared, and it could not occur as it does if that were not the case.' If you had written to a black friend, even in the course of a correspondence which had set out to investigate differences between black and white people, that the differences between black and white people 'can only be described as vast', that it is an 'elemental' truth that what white people prefer above all else in life is a kind of experience from which black people are necessarily excluded, and that this experience is 'foundational to ordinary living', wouldn't you expect your friend to be surprised and to say that what you had written at least *sounded* racist, or at least like a defence of segregationism?

In my reply I explained that I was surprised by these passages in your letter because 'they *looked* to me *like* an emphatic re-assertion of the old "isolationist" [I should have said "segregationist"] view'. Admittedly the words I have put in italics now were not in italics originally, but I went on: '*Probably they were not meant to be* that' (italics again introduced by me now) 'but in order not to serve as a justification for the revival of what I believe to have been very bad old ways, they would need at least to be seriously qualified.' From that I think it is reasonably

clear that what I was asserting was *not* that you held segregationist views, but that what you had said might unintentionally
serve as a justification for such views. Now it has surely often
happened that the very best of people have from time to time
said things which have turned out to have, or at least to be
plausibly interpretable as having, implications which they
would wish to repudiate when they became aware of them.
And it is everywhere acknowledged to be a proper mode of
procedure in discussion to point to what you believe to be
implications of a view which its proponent might not want to
accept, as a way of persuading him to abandon or modify the
view. That was what I was doing. Far from suspecting that you
were a segregationist, I was assuming that you were not, and
that you would therefore want to modify or amplify what you
had said.

That is what you have done, in fact. In Letter 6 you make it
clear that by 'ordinary living' you mean life as lived by sighted
people when interacting with one another, from which blind
people are excluded only by definition – a possible interpretation of your words which I had explicitly envisaged in Letter 4 –
and, very importantly, you indicate clearly that you agree that
blind people can 'communicate with others in a wide range of
ways, including some of the most subtle, and relate to them on a
wide variety of bases, including the most intimate, by other
means'. If blind people can communicate with sighted people in
'some of the most subtle' ways and 'relate to them on a wide
variety of bases, including the most intimate' by other means –
which, for that to happen, must be accessible to sighted as well
as blind people – I find it hard to understand why one should
say that visual experience is 'foundational' to ordinary living.
For it would seem to follow that sighted people can enter into
the same sort of relationships with blind people as they can with

one another, but without the mediation of sight; and that therefore the mediation of sight may not be so essential to their relationships with one another as it is sometimes, understandably, thought to be. But in any case these amplifications by you of what you said in Letter 3 certainly carry forward our discussion, and reduce my fear – as does much else which you have written in Letter 6 – that segregationists and visionists might find some comfort in what you say. Any worries I still have about what you say on these matters are not and never have been that you are either a segregationist or a visionist (which by the way are not in my view the same thing, although they are closely linked).

That I never suspected you of being a visionist I think I made quite clear in that paragraph of my Letter 4 which began: 'I certainly do not think that you are a visionist'. It is true that in that paragraph I gave only one of my reasons for my confidence on this matter, but that was because I thought the single reason I gave was sufficient by itself to put that question beyond dispute. Again in this paragraph I explicitly invited you to consider whether the part of your letter under discussion 'hasn't at least the *appearance* of being a bit visionist' (italics in this case in the original), and I asked whether you would want to modify (as I was sure you would) the views stated there.

You might reply that all the same I did say that you were exaggerating the extent of the differences there are between blind and sighted people, and that by my definition of 'visionism' you have to be a visionist, whatever I may have said to the contrary. I certainly did think that you exaggerated the differences between blind and sighted people, and so there would be force in this; but what was wrong in my last letter was not that I expressed unjust suspicions about you but that my proffered definition of visionism did not properly express my actual notion of it. My explanation of what I meant by 'vision-ism' would more accurately have reflected how I actually use the word if I had said that it was an exaggeration of the differences between sighted and blind people, with a one-sided emphasis on the (real and supposed) advantages and superiori-ties of the sighted over the blind, proceeding from or resulting in some lack of respect for, and fellow-feeling with, blind people.

Apart from that I am aware only of one thing in my Letter 4 for which I feel I have to apologise. That is the paragraph in which I likened you to a missionary preaching the gospel of sight to the blind in outer darkness. That, I'm afraid, was nothing better than some knock-about debating, which I thought of as a bit of fun at the time, but in which I was inexcusably rough with you and which, on re-reading, I can well understand your being hurt by. For that I sincerely and unreservedly apologise.

Incidentally, you were wrong in suggesting that in Letter 4 I questioned your motives in writing about the differences be-tween blind and sighted people. I nowhere did so, and I would not need to, for you have been quite frank from the beginning about the fact that at least a major part of your motivation in writing about it is that you want through that to make a general philosophical point about the nature of the knowledge any human being can have of the real world. I have no difficulty at all in accepting that this is your major motive, or in accepting that the asperity which you admit was present in a passage in Letter 3 arose from a philosophical conviction of yours which you have had to fight for over and over again. I am not a philosophical idealist, but I do believe that philosophical ideas can quite often act as powerful immediate causes of specific acts and beliefs.

II   Grieving for the Loss of Sight

The second misunderstanding about what I wrote in Letter 4 which I must not leave without comment is contained in your idea in Letter 6 that, when I said that large numbers of recently-blind people are disproportionately depressed or damaged in spirit as a result of the widespread exaggeration of the importance of sight, I was offering an explanation of all the grief people feel when they lose their sight. That is not what I was doing. In my very next sentence I say: 'Loss of sight cannot and should not be experienced as anything other than a serious loss'. And a little later on I say that, for some people – those who have 'lived in their eyes' – it is perhaps inevitable that loss of sight should be experienced as 'cataclysmic'. I have been very close to someone of this second kind whose sudden blindness was an exceptionally heavy and enduring blow, as well as to people for whom loss of sight has been less traumatic but still very depressing, and I have shared their grief. There is plenty to grieve over in the loss of sight, even for those who do not exaggerate its importance. I myself was grief-stricken when I was unexpectedly told by doctors that my baby son, who could see perfectly well at the time, would almost certainly soon be blind, and I have never ceased to be grateful to that doctor and to the National Health Service generally for managing to stop that coming about. You were wrong, therefore, when you said 'The recently-blind know what they have lost. You do not.' You were making the same error as you made when you said that born-blind people cannot know what they are missing.

In the passage you quoted from me, as I say, I was not seeking to explain the grief that anyone must feel if they lose such a precious thing as their sight. That hardly seemed to need explaining, or even anything beyond the briefest acknowledgement by me, after all I had said in Letter 4 in support of the view that blindness is a major handicap. What I was trying to do in the part of my letter where the passage which you quoted occurs was to make four other points. The first was that although sight is precious, it is possible to exaggerate its importance in human life. The second was that it is very easy for sighted people to do this because of the enormous extent to which they actually use sight. The third was that it is harmful to do this, in part because of the harm that is done to already-blind people through the consequent under-estimation of the value of the help they could receive, and by the constant, widespread under-rating of their capacities. And the fourth was that it is also harmful because many of the sighted people in whose minds this exaggeration is, as it were, naturally lodged will themselves eventually become blind, and many of these are likely to be, I repeat, disproportionately depressed or damaged in spirit when this happens. Although they have genuinely suffered a serious loss, their exaggerated notions of the loss they have suffered will make things worse than they need be.

You deny this. 'On the contrary, you say, 'it is clear to me that the mourning is proportionate to the loss, and that this is why it occurs.' You say that this is clear to you. But how can it be? How can you know that it is always proportionate? In Letter 4 I asked you if your view is that the importance of sight is such that it is simply impossible to exaggerate it. I still do not know your answer to that question. I would be glad to know it – and now, also, to know if you think that it is just impossible to be too depressed by the loss of sight, or to be damaged in spirit, or to avoid being damaged in spirit. My guess is that you had just been reading Hull's book, in particular his description of the deep crisis into which he was plunged by the loss of sight; and that you thought: 'No, Hull's depression and sense of disorientation were not disproportionate but entirely appropriate, even if they included for a time some unrealistic worries and fears'. I entirely agree about that. Hull's depression was not disproportionate, nor was he unnecessarily damaged in spirit by his loss of sight. Although the onset of blindness brought him stresses and anxieties of various kinds, and moments of despair, he did not despair to the point of giving up trying to move about by himself, giving up his job, and giving up his role as a father. But how do you know that that is true of everyone or nearly everyone who has become blind? You can't know that, because it isn't. In the quarter of a century and more during which I have been working closely with blind people I have known many recently-blind people who have been just like John Hull in this respect: they have not lost their spirit, or given up on life, although they went through periods of severe depression and anxiety. But I have also known quite a few who resigned from their jobs when they needn't have done, stopped making any effort to get about by themselves, even within their own homes, and abandoned all their social responsibilities; and thus – for some considerable time, at least, and sometimes for life – gave up the attempt to live their own life, either completely or, at any rate, to an extent beyond what their condition required. It would be absurd to say that in all cases this was entirely due to the view they held about the importance of sight; but it would also be absurd, I think, to assert that the view they had held, as sighted people – that sight is essential to doing all but a tiny number of jobs, to getting about by oneself, and generally to handling responsibilities competently – a view which of course was not likely to vanish from their minds the moment they themselves were overtaken by blindness, had nothing to do with the excessive despair to which they succumbed when they became blind.

In Letter 4 I did not ask you to accept this as simply my judgement. I told you, for instance, about the group near Leeds which has chosen to call itself VINE – Vision Is Not Essential. This group is entirely composed of people who have quite recently lost their sight (of them and some of their close relatives), a hundred or more, mostly in late middle age or older. Their principal aim is to bring information and encouragement to other newly-blind people. The name they have chosen for their group is controversial, because vision is essential for some things that some recently-blind people would still like to do. But they have chosen it because, in some cases after prolonged periods of blank despair and of 'feeling useless', as they put it, they have made the heartening discovery that vision is not essential to living full, useful and enjoyable lives, even as members of predominantly sighted communities. They send this message because they believe that many newly-blind people are inclined, as they themselves were, to exaggerate the importance of sight and its loss. While making this point they also stress, as I would, that blind people living in predominantly sighted communities do need special help of various kinds in coping with their handicap, and that even with help they cannot satisfactorily solve all the problems they encounter. Nevertheless they take the view that lack of information about what blind people can do, and about what help is available to them if they know how to get it, has unnecessarily, excessively and damagingly depressed many newly-blind people. These views are certainly shared by large numbers of become-blind people everywhere in this country, and by many sighted people who work with and for blind people.

I do not think they think of loss of sight as exactly comparable to loss of a loved one. This analogy was fashionable not long ago among some social workers for the blind. Some blind people have thought it illuminating, partly because it is (sometimes rightly) thought that particular newly-blind people could benefit from a type of 'bereavement counselling'; but the idea of loss of sight being very similar to loss of a loved one has never been really popular among either blind people or even the majority of people working with them. VINE in their earlier literature (I have not seen their most recent productions) do not ask at all for counselling, but exclusively for practical information and support.

The reason why a majority of become-blind people, in my experience, do not think of the loss of sight as being quite like the loss of a loved friend is, I believe, this. To love a person is not merely to think of that person as very useful, or even as a source of many pleasures: it is to feel that the person is precious in himself or herself, as an individual, irrespective of usefulness or consequences; so that if he or she dies we have to grieve for a loss that we know will never be made good, although no doubt in time we shall get used to it. The majority of blind people who have talked to me about loss of sight, on the other hand, have not talked of it in that way. The loss of sight has been a bitter blow to them, to a large extent (I do not say wholly) because of what they have thought of, often unfortunately quite rightly, as losses that go with it: loss of job, severe loss of income, loss of respect from people around them, above all loss of independence and control. If they then find that these other losses can be made good, as they certainly can and sometimes are, and that many of the benefits that came through sight can be got in other ways, then their sense of loss is at least very greatly diminished. I repeat that I am not claiming this to be true of all become-blind people. Some do grieve for their sight as for a loved friend, having experienced seeing, when they were sighted, not just as useful but as intensely desirable in itself, and even perhaps occasionally as something for which they had a constant craving, as you describe so vividly in Letter 6. But from my conversations with scores of become-blind people I would say that those who intensely loved seeing for its own sake are a minority. Whenever I have asked: 'What do you miss, now that you are blind?' the overwhelming majority have replied by mentioning practical things – things they cannot do, or think they cannot do. I believe that loss of the pleasures of sight is nearly always an element in their total sense of loss, sometimes quite an important element, but I think that I myself may have exaggerated this point a bit towards the end of Letter 5 – because, come to think of it, loss of these pleasures is sometimes not mentioned at all by recently-blind people. (If mentioned, it is usually as a subsidiary element in their total sense of loss.)

My wife Joan, who thinks she may now be close to the point of losing her sight completely, says that one effect of approaching this point has been suddenly to sharpen the pleasure she gets from looking at flowers and landscapes – but that the fear of losing these pleasures is dwarfed by other fears: the fear of not being able to get about safely by herself, of not being able to do her own shopping (already very difficult), of not being able to cook in the way she likes, of needing the kind of help that for years she has herself been giving to other totally blind people. She fears these things even although she knows a lot about what totally blind people can do, and about how much help is available. She fears them for the reason I have already given – that, although her sight has been very poor for most of her life, she has been, and still is, so dependent on it. 'But if she still has these fears even with the knowledge you want people to have,' you may ask, 'what good is the knowledge?' The good, I believe, is that if total blindness does come to her, although she will be enormously stressed and depressed, she will not give in.

Because she knows others have succeeded she is the more likely to struggle to keep control of her life. If she struggles, precedent suggests she will succeed. When she becomes more dependent on the help of others she will learn for herself that if this is given in the way she herself has given it for so long the receiving of help need not hurt and can be compatible with remaining in control. She will learn that there are many people like herself who genuinely want to give help of that kind, and that if help of that kind is not available, humiliating and hurtful help can be done without, or in extremity endured, without in either case her being humiliated, losing ultimate control or losing her integrity – without her ceasing to be a person. It will surely be easier for her to learn that if she has already known many totally blind people who have demonstrated its truth, and therefore the truth that sight is not 'foundational' to what most people would think of as most important in ordinary living.

III   Differences in Experience: Dreams

But it is time now to fulfil the promise made early in this letter. As the text for most of the rest of this letter I shall take this sentence of yours from Letter 6: 'What we should both be trying to do at this stage is identify and bring out clearly some of the crucial experiential differences between the sighted and the blind as a preliminary to asking what further differences these in their turn make to the concepts we form' and initially, since otherwise it would be question-begging, I shall understand the phrase 'the crucial experiential differences' as being short for 'what might be thought to be the crucial experiential differences', leaving open to begin with the question of whether there is anything to which such differences are crucial, and if so what it is. I shall also bear in mind the questions you ask near the beginning and the end of Letter 7. In discussing these questions I shall be primarily concerned with my own experience as a person without visual experience, and without any memory of visual experience. But to bring out how much blind as well as sighted people can differ among themselves I shall also refer from time to time not only to what John Hull says but also to differences between me and other blind people who, like me, have no memory of visual experience. Let me start with dreams and sleep.

Like you, I have frequently been struck by the fact that it is blind people's dreams that seem particularly to excite the interest of sighted people. Why don't they ask about my waking experience, I sometimes wonder. And why, when I have explained that my dreamt perceptions are mostly quite like my waking perceptions (as I suppose theirs are) have they seemed somehow dissatisfied and baffled – so much so that I don't even say that now, at least to begin with. I think that what you say about the special vividness of some sighted people's dreams may be part of the explanation, but I'm not sure it tells the whole story. At any rate, what I now say to such people, and will say here, is: Yes, I think I dream most nights. And though I forget most of my dreams very soon after waking, and without recording them, some of my dreams, or at least some bits of them, stay with me for a long time. And no, I don't ever dream that I am seeing anything. But I do sometimes dream that I am holding or touching something or someone. I sometimes dream that I am hearing voices or sounds. I invariably dream that I have some awareness of my environment through that other kind of 'hearing' of what is silent, which I was so delighted to learn you could recognise from your own childhood experiences. My dreams also frequently include some awareness of my body, and of how I am moving, the kind of awareness associated with kinaesthetic sensations. But in my dreams it is very rare for sensory awareness of any kind to be prominent. What is normally in the foreground of my dreams – at least as I remember them even the moment I wake from them, with my dreamed sensory awareness present only as background, or as material for, or at most as stimulus to, this – is my dreamt thinking and feeling about what is going on in the dream.

To give some examples. A dream which I have had a few times in recent years is that I am in a lift which I know well in the Arts Building of Leeds University, and that I am going up in it, usually with other people. When it reaches the top floor it does not stop and open its doors as it would in waking life, but changes its motion from an upward motion to a motion in a horizontal plane, taking us, sometimes after quite a ride that includes some turns, into another building, where it stops and lets us out. We are all surprised by this, but not panicked. In some later occurrences of the dream I am less surprised than the others because, having dreamt this dream before, I think I already know that this lift can do this sort of thing. Although the Arts Building in real life is connected with another building, and that in turn with another, the building we come into from the lift does not seem familiar, and I usually seem to feel baffled about where I am – and wake up. Now, how do I know that I am in the lift? Not by seeing or even, usually, touching what surrounds me. Even if I did this it wouldn't tell me that I was in the lift in the Arts Building of the University. But I seem to remember getting into that particular lift, and my 'object-sense' in the dream (just as in waking life) seems to confirm that I am in a confined space of about the right size for that lift. How do I know that we are going up and then changing motion? As in my waking life, not by looking at a lighted panel but from the pressure on my feet exerted by an upward-moving body diminishing, and then changing to the sensation of moving in a level plane, such as one gets whilst standing in a moving underground train. How do I know the others in the lift are surprised? Not by looking at their faces, and not because they are talking much (in the dream silence prevails, for the most part) but from little sounds that they make, changes in the sound of their breathing, or slight exclamations, all as in waking life. And how do I know that I am in an unfamiliar building? Not because it looks unfamiliar, but because the sensations from my feet, my kinaesthetic sensations, the way the sound of my footsteps is echoed, other sounds in the air, and above all the 'sound-shadows' given off (and not given off) by my surroundings, all combine to make this place feel unfamiliar, different in small but significant ways from the feel of any other building I can remember. But, as in waking life, none of this is in the forefront of my attention. To begin with, as we go up in the lift, I am thinking about the people I am expecting to meet in the School of History on the top floor, and perhaps also wondering about who else is in the lift. Later I start wondering about what has happened, where we are going to, etc. It is these thinkings and wonderings, and feelings of slight unease, mixed with excitement and pleasure at the novel, which dominate my non-visual 'dream-scene'. Although there may seem to be some rather obvious symbolism in this dream (perhaps it is a pre- and immediate post-retirement dream) I don't feel that I really know what it is 'about'. When I wake from it I wake feeling that it was a rather pleasant and interesting dream, but not that it was a very important one, although its repetition should perhaps warn me to take it a bit more seriously.

A dream which I did take very seriously when I awoke from it, and have always subsequently remembered as exceptionally significant, was one I had as I was approaching the age of thirty.

Letter 8

In this dream I found myself swimming in the North Sea in a southerly direction, parallel to the east coast of England but a few miles, I thought, out to sea. At that time in real life I was a reasonably good indoor swimming-bath swimmer, but had had little experience of swimming in the sea. In my dream I felt some anxiety at being out at sea, and wondered where I would get to, and even vaguely how I had got where I was; but there seemed to be nothing for it but to keep on swimming. Eventually I came to what I believed was the Thames Estuary. I turned right up the estuary, and after a while right again into a tributary. I swam up that, and up smaller tributaries, until I found myself in a small brook which was too shallow to swim in. At first I felt relieved to be in these narrower waters, but eventually this turned to severe disappointment. When I awoke from this dream, which was one of the most vivid I have ever had, I seemed to know immediately that this had said something very important to me. It wasn't long before I thought I knew what that was. At the time of the dream I had been unemployed for several years after a prolonged and fairly hectic period at university, and I was living back with my parents in the very pleasant small country town where I had spent the later part of my childhood. I had tried very hard to get jobs teaching philosophy, but I hadn't tried hard for any other kind of job, because if I got one my chances of getting the philosophy work I really wanted to do might be reduced – and although I'd been registered for work for several years, and had indicated that I would consider anything, I had never been offered, or invited to apply for, any job. This dream seemed to me a clear message from myself to myself that it was time to get out into the world of work, whatever the work and whatever the effort it might cost to get there. And I acted accordingly.

My memory of this dream is even now quite vivid. It is a vivid memory of a dream which was itself, as I have said, very vivid, in the sense that it took possession of me whilst I was dreaming it and afterwards to an exceptional degree. But the sensory content of the dream was not vivid: indeed, there was hardly any, other than the dreamt kinaesthetic sensations associated with the movements of swimming; and the sense, resulting from there being no sound-shadows, of there being unlimited space in the sea. You might have expected me to dream that I was feeling cold in the sea, or to dream that after a swim of several miles I would feel tired; but I didn't. How I knew, or rather why I believed, that it was the North Sea in which I was swimming, the dream did not make clear – nor why I believed that I was a few miles out from the English coast – nor why I believed that I had come to the Thames Estuary (about which, I seem to remember, I was initially in some doubt, though later the sounds of my surroundings as I raised my head out of the water from time to time assured me that I had come in from the open sea). What was in the centre of my dream was not sensory detail, or how I knew what I knew, but the story-line, i.e. what I knew, or more precisely the thought-content of the dream – what I believed was happening, and (very important to the significance of the dream, I believe, despite what some psychologists say about that) how I felt about it. In this again, it seems to me, my dream was quite like my waking life. For there it is often the case that my beliefs about where I am (in space and time) and about what I am doing, and about what is going on around me, are not predominantly determined by the sensory content of my immediate experience. That plays a part, of course, but often only by conforming sufficiently to already-formed beliefs and expectations to allow them to stand – a role it can perform very unobtrusively in the margin of my attention, as it were. How do I come by already-formed beliefs and expectations? Often I do not think about this, and when I do I cannot immediately say. Memories of where I have been in the recent past, and what I have done and planned, often play a determining role, I am sure. And of course in the establishment of some of these memories direct sense-perception is likely to have played a prominent part. But the point I am making is that in waking life I often have beliefs about what is going on which are not actively generated by my present perceptual experience, or by anything else of which I am immediately conscious, so it is not surprising if in dreams I often seem to know things without knowing how.

I would expect this to be true to some extent of other people, sighted as well as blind. But perhaps not of all to the same extent as in my case, for the reason that sight is in a special degree an attention-demanding and attention-commanding sense. Sighted people, as you say, constantly want to look, and it seems to be more difficult (though by no means impossible of course) to ignore what one sees than it is to ignore the messages of other senses. It is more difficult to close one's ears, or to close off one's kinaesthetic sensations, than it is to close one's eyes, but just for that reason, perhaps, we get into the way of ignoring or almost ignoring more of the messages of these other senses. This is true, I think, even of the born-blind, or at least of some of us. I was surprised that you were surprised by the point that blind people may think more than sighted people, on average. Sighted people have constantly sought to comfort me, and perhaps themselves, by saying that I am able to think more because I am less distracted by the senses. I'm afraid I used to dismiss this with the argument that since blind people have to attend more than sighted people to what the other senses say (which is true), they can be just as distracted by them as sighted people are by sight. I have come to think that although that conclusion may be true of some blind people it need not be true of all, and in fact it is not true of me: these other senses are not inherently such attention-grabbers as sight seems to be. But if it is true that I and some other blind people are inclined to spend a greater part of our time 'thinking', because less dominated by our senses, it need not follow that this thinking is necessarily anything very elevated, like rigorous reasoning, or concentrated meditation. It *can* be that; but it can also be – and in me too often is – just uncreative day-dreaming, or a train of loosely-associated ideas getting nowhere.

If I am right about the especially intrusive character of sight, that may explain why people who can see, or who have had sight, dream of seeing with an intensity not paralleled by the imagery from other senses in the dreams of people like me. It is not that dreams always copy waking life: they don't, not always. People who have had sight but have lost it long since have ceased to see anything in their waking lives, but some of them tell me that they go on seeing things in their dreams, sometimes very vividly (and Hull of course describes this). Rather, I think, it is that people who have sight, or have had sight, have got so used to having their beliefs checked by sight, with or against their will, that when they are asleep their minds need to manufacture visual images in order that they will be gripped by the stories which their fears and desires are making them tell themselves – whereas for people like me, not constantly forced to attend to our sensory images in waking life, the mere absence of such images that sleep brings is often of itself enough to allow us to be possessed by the stories our minds spin. At any rate it does seem to be the case, from what they say, that the dreams of people who have sight, or who have had sight, are more dominated by visual images than mine are by any images. Certainly I don't have 'hyper-vivid' images of any

197

kind in my dreams comparable to the images you speak of sighted people having in theirs.

As to the questions you have asked about the dreams of blind people, it is, as I have just indicated, not the imagery but the story that grips me in my dreams – just as when listening to a gripping radio play, or reading a gripping novel, one's mind is with the action or the emotions portrayed, not at all with the sensory inputs through which one receives the portrayal. That at least is my experience. And it seems to be true of some other born-blind people – I am not sure if it is true of all. I suppose blind people talk as much or as little about their dreams as do sighted people, but I don't know of any special common stock of beliefs about dreams among them. Quite a number of totally blind people do seem to believe that we are especially apt to suffer from insomnia, and that this is due to the fact that we lack the trigger to sleep which the change from light to darkness supplies to those with sight. I don't know about that. My own insomnia has often taken the form of waking early rather than failing to get to sleep.

John Hull writes a lot, and fascinatingly, about his dreams. As was to be expected in a grown man subjected to the recent trauma of loss of sight, many of the dreams he describes seem to be about his blindness, and to express the intense anxieties to which it has given rise in him. Although blindness has been a source of some important practical and social problems for me, it has never, as far as I can remember, been the source of the trauma, anxieties and despair to which he was subject. Any problems I may have had as an infant in adjusting to being blind after having had sight seem to have left no trace in me. Of course, as you say, infant experiences that are not remembered may nevertheless have lifelong effects; but I don't have any evidence of loss of sight having been experienced by me as a terrible blow or a devastating deprivation. I don't remember losing my sight, or any shock or disturbance which I can identify as related to that; and from what my parents and others have said, blindness just did not seem to be a problem for me as a young child. I took it for granted, and learned to live with it. Other people who have been totally blind since infancy say the same about their early childhood. Later in my boyhood I longed to be better at football than my blindness permitted. Later still, as I have mentioned, I thought for a while that my blindness was getting in the way of the sort of relationships with some girls that I wanted to have. All through my life blindness has made getting about more of a strain than I would have wished. I think it has made advanced study and some other things more difficult than they would have been otherwise. But I don't think the issue of blindness ever went deep enough to get into my dreams. For as long as I can remember I have been blind, and at home with my blindness.

As it happens, the very earliest dream that I can remember, like one of Hull's most striking fantasies, was about a tunnel, but it was about my coming out of a tunnel, not going into one. I remember that when I awoke from it I felt a very special kind of happiness at the memory of the dream. I was only four at the time, but I seem to remember myself lying in bed after waking and thinking: 'This is the happiest I have ever been'. I did not dream of coming out of the tunnel as being a transition from darkness to light, of course, but as being a transition from a shut-in, cut-off condition resulting from the close presence of thick walls casting their sound-shadows, and excluding sounds from outside, to being out in the open, free of sound-shadows. I am not inclined to accept the interpretation, which some might suggest, that this was a dream about emerging from the womb, at least not this as being the most important level at which the dream had meaning for me when I dreamt it. Part of my present memory of that dream is actually a memory of remembering it later, of sitting in my school-room just after I had begun to go to school, at the age of five, and remembering this dream as being one I had had just before I was five. I felt that it was a 'big' dream, and that it was about some sort of understanding that had come to me. Although I knew I had had the dream before being at school, I felt on that morning that it had been a sort of foreshadowing of my coming to school – something I experienced as a great freeing up and filling out of my life. The dream seemed to say that I had got, or was getting, some kind of control of things that I hadn't had before. Retrospectively I associate it with the attainment of a level of selfconsciousness not previously there. But I have never thought of it as being about, or as being related to, my blindness.

In many of my dreams I am aware that I am blind while others around can see. But this is a straightforward, unemotional awareness of a fact, like my awareness of being male, not an awareness of something to be feared or resented or mourned. In contrast to Hull, I can't remember ever having a dream which seemed to have my blindness as its central theme.

IV   Differences in Experience: Waking Life
Time And Space

Differences between John Hull's response to being blind and mine, in waking life as well as in our dreams, are of course to be expected. Not only had he been blind for less than three years when he began to write his book (and for less than six when he finished it), whereas I have been blind for well over sixty years; more significantly, he became totally and permanently blind after living for forty-five years as a sighted person, with the ingrained habits and expectations and memories of a sighted person, whereas I was only eighteen months old and relatively unformed when I became blind. I have been astonished at the speed with which he has learnt many of the things a blind person has to learn, delighted at the number of times I have been able to say, 'Yes, that's just how it's been for me too!'. All the same, there are quite a lot of differences between our experiences of blindness; and I think I have to deal with these in the course of bringing out the differences (and samenesses) between my experience and that of sighted people, because you have, understandably, been so impressed by Hull's book.

One set of differences between Hull and me relates to our experience of time and space. He sums up his experience by saying that for a blind person there is more time and less space than for sighted people, whereas I have to say that neither part of that statement is true in my case – nor, I think, in the case of a number of other blind people I know. It is understandable that Hull should think he has more time than he had when he was sighted, because by his own account he gave up many commitments when he lost his sight to concentrate on essential tasks. It is also probable – I suppose, though he hints at this only indirectly – that his new wife took over sole responsibility for a number of tasks that he might have been expected to share if he had not lost his sight. But since it is true, as he says, that many tasks are bound to take blind people longer than they would sighted people, the question of whether you have more time as a blind person would seem to depend entirely on how good you are at judging what you can do in a given time, how free you are to cut out tasks you think you should cut out, and how strong-minded you are about doing it. If, as Hull tells us, he seemed to a close colleague to have more time for the things he had to do than anyone else in his faculty, that is a testimony to his good judgement, self-discipline and perhaps good luck. But it has, I think, nothing to do with his blindness, except that its onset, as any major change in one's condition might, precipitated a review by him of how he should spend his time – and no doubt an upsurge of willingness among friends and colleagues to help out in various ways. Hull's explanation of his own appearance of being unhurried – that blind people simply cannot hurry the things they do – has some truth, for there are some things that blind people can't hurry in the way that sighted people can. But the implications of this fact would seem to be that blind people would have less and not more time to spare as compared with sighted people, unless they sharply reduce their expectations of themselves (which not all blind people are equally willing to do). In any case it seems obvious that, even when doing things that they cannot hurry, some people, blind or sighted, can feel and appear flustered, far from having plenty of time to spare. Hull is clearly a very well-organised, clear-headed and energetic person. When he was sighted, perhaps he took on more than he could comfortably manage. But when he became blind he would think it important to be realistic about what he could do, and must have judged this well. He cannot attribute this to his blindness, however, for if that were responsible, all blind people would at the very least have a strong tendency to be, and to appear to be, unhurried, as if they have plenty of time for what they have to do. Many do, of course – partly because the unnecessarily high levels of unemployment, poverty and isolation among blind people mean that the only thing many of them have much of is free time. But that is by no means true of all blind people. Quite a number, both young and old, have a lot to do. Amongst these, some take on only as much as they can easily manage without hurry or strain. Others take on more than they can easily manage, but by a combination of good judgement and good organisation appear most of the time to have plenty of time. And others still, including me, take on more than they can easily manage, and show the strain.

During most of my life I have kept biting off more than I could chew. When I was young I became notorious for frequently being late for appointments. In later life I tried to get rid of that reputation, with perhaps some success. But I have never been good at judging how long particular tasks would take me, have constantly been over-ambitious, over-optimistic about what I could accomplish in a given time, and have frequently lacked the strength of mind to eschew tasks which such judgement as I have warned me against undertaking. In consequence, I have constantly both been and appeared to be short of time. If there are some blind people who have or appear to have more time at their disposal than many sighted people, there are certainly many sighted people who have or appear to have far more time at their disposal than I normally have.

Four years ago, when I retired from paid work, I had to have major heart surgery. When I was recovering from that I was, for a while, so weak that I had to withdraw from almost all my commitments. During that period I did feel that I had some time to spare – and what a luxurious feeling that was! But gradually I got involved in things again. Now I'm nearly as pressed for time as ever. You yourself have had experience of my old failings. I don't want to give a false picture of myself as a busy, energetic person. Compared with many blind and sighted people I know I'm not at all that. Like my father (who was not blind) I tend to do everything I do (except talking) very slowly, and since I have a very low energy-level I take many breaks from what I am doing. I therefore may not always appear to others to be very busy, but to those who know me at all intimately I do appear to be, what I am, constantly anxious about the passage of time and my ever-pressing lack of it. Of course I don't think that that arises from blindness, any more than I think that Hull's sense of the abundance of time does. In fact, I don't think there's any regular causal relation between blindness and awareness of the amount of time at one's disposal, nor can I see why there should be any.

'But isn't Hull right in suggesting that a totally blind person's experience of the passage of time is different from that of sighted people in that it lacks punctuation?' Certainly it lacks some particular punctuation marks, such as the waxing and waning of daylight, the browning of the leaves in autumn, the green shoots of spring. But other 'natural' punctuation is still there for blind people: the swings of temperature through day and night, the seasons, the crunch or mush of the fallen leaves underfoot, the singing and silences of the birds. And of course blind people share that punctuation which bulks so much larger than natural punctuation in the lives of the great majority of sighted people in present-day, clock-regulated, urbanised society, the punctuation constituted by the hours at which you start and stop work, go to concerts or a pub, have to keep appointments, have to get the last bus home, the punctuation of working week and weekend, school-terms and holidays, the times of regular television and radio programmes. Which particular punctuation marks in one's experience are important varies according to one's interests and activities – but not at all, as far as I can see, according to whether one has or has not got sight. The fact that John Hull and I know the time by the press of a button on our talking watches, rather than by glancing at the watch dial, is surely a tiny and immaterial difference between us and sighted people compared with the sameness that we all want to know, and can easily know, clock time. That sighted people have access to more additional indications of the passage of time than blind people is, though not insignificant from every point of view, not very important, I would think, from the point of view of our sense of how much time we have.

With regard to the perception of the passage of time there may be one difference between totally blind people and people with sight which could be significant. I read a popular science article recently which suggested that our body-clocks, which control various automatic processes within our bodies, may tend to run slightly slow, and that it is the perception of light which corrects them. If in this regard light can, as I suppose, affect human beings only through their eyes, does this mean that totally blind people's body-clocks don't get corrected, or at least run a bit differently from other people's? Could this account for the difficulties many of us have in getting regular sleep? This might be a topic worth some research. Failing that, I don't know of any significant difference with regard to the perception of time between blind and sighted people as such. Nor, therefore, do I think there is likely to be any systematic difference between our conceptions of, or beliefs about, time. I agree with Kant that time is the form of all our sensory awareness. But I think it is so because, as Engels says, it is one of the forms, or part of the form, of everything that exists. I don't agree that Kant has shown in his Antinomies that this is something we can't rationally believe. I therefore can't make any sense of talk *à la* Wells or Dunne about travelling backwards or forwards through time, or about different time-dimensions, or about the beginning of time, or histories of time, or reversals of time, however eminent the physicists who go in for such talk – other than as rather slipshod ways of saying that certain specific events, or sorts of events, have preceded, or followed, or happened simultaneously with others. But since this incapacity of mine seems to be shared by a number of sighted people whose minds I very much respect I don't think this is a blind/sighted issue, nor do I expect that you will want to hear any more about it from me.

It might seem that Hull's contention that blind people have less space than sighted people relates to the fact that many blind people are relatively immobile, being limited to the confines of their own room or to a very restricted area. But it would be a mistake to think of such limitations as being imposed by their blindness, for such limitations are imposed primarily by their poverty or lack of support. If they could afford to use taxis frequently, or have paid assistants to accompany them wherever they want to go, as well-off blind people can, they could get about more than many poor sighted people. But Hull does not make this mistake. It would be surprising if he did, because – partly because of exceptional courage in his case, and partly, no doubt, because even blind professors aren't too badly off – he seems to have continued to travel about quite a lot after the onset of total blindness, not only within his own city but throughout the British Isles, and even to Australia and Canada. Alternatively, you might think that what he means by saying that blind people have less space than sighted people is just that blind people's perception of their surroundings generally extends much less far, and is much less detailed, than sighted people's. If that were what he meant I wouldn't want to disagree with him, because I'm sure it's true. Indeed, I have already said that to you in an earlier letter. This would surely be an odd way, though, of expressing some simple truths, and in fact I believe that what Hull chiefly has in mind is something else – which I can readily accept reflects something in his experience, but again not in mine.

Letter 9

FROM BRYAN MAGEE
TO THE READER

At the point where Letter 8 breaks off, Martin was taken ill. His illness proved to be serious, and he had to have a drastic operation. Not long after it he realized he was dying. He faced death with courage but not with resignation: he was enraged that this should be happening to him at such an inconvenient time, when he had so many other things to do. But his bravery could not alter reality, and within weeks of having been taken ill he died. The suddenness of it all made the shock worse for his family and those closest to him. Among the many losses caused by his unexpected death is the continuation of this correspondence.

From the beginning of our discussion Martin had run off with it in a direction I had not anticipated, and could not possibly have anticipated, because he mounted assaults on positions I did not occupy. So I cannot predict how he would have continued. And I must leave it to readers to judge for them-selves the merits of our arguments as we have advanced them up to this point. I do not propose now to bring forward any new arguments against positions occupied by Martin. To continue those disputes further would be one-sided now that he is no longer able to reply, and indeed would be unfair to him. I shall leave his last letter unanswered, and thus leave him with the last word on all the matters with which it deals. However, at the very beginning of the correspondence I raised certain questions and said they were among my basic reasons for launching the whole thing, yet they were not followed up in the arguments between us. But because they were why I started it all in the first place I want to say something about them before finishing. I have no idea how Martin would have responded to what I am going to say. No doubt he would have disagreed with it. If I am asked why in that case I say it here and not elsewhere my answer is the twofold one that I want the things I say to be read in the light of many of the points established in this correspondence, and that they are what I was groping my way towards through our preliminary discussions. In putting them to the reader now I invite his critical consideration of them exactly as I would have done Martin's.

Although Martin never got as far as considering the first questions I raised, it is not the case that he did not illuminate them for me. He illuminated them not by what he said but by what he did. The reader will agree, I am sure, that he showed the deepest possible reluctance, frequently crossing the border-line into refusal, to go along with any view to the effect that his lack of visual experience radically impoverished the conception he had of reality. On the contrary, he was insistent that he could know everything I could know, and do most of what I could do. So what else was left, he wanted to know? Not all that much, in his opinion. My answer was that the entire world as visually experienced was left plus most of what can follow from the having of that experience. But this did not cut much ice with him. He was convinced that the sighted were blowing up what were often (not always) minor differences into major ones, to the point of unjust discrimination against the blind; and his chief concern was to rectify what he considered this misconception and the resultant injustices.

Watching these processes at work in him led me to a breakthrough in my understanding of what some of the probable consequences for me are of the limitations inherent in my own equipment. Obviously these do not embrace the frontier between being blind and being sighted, but I came more and more to use that distinction as I saw it operating in Martin as an indication of the probable workings of my own sensory limitations, especially in their effect on the formation of my general conception of reality.

What I would like to do, then, is to round this volume off by putting some of these considerations before the reader. From the beginning they have been what I most wanted to get into, and would have written about anyway as our correspondence continued. But from this point onwards neither blindness nor the blind/sighted distinction are *in themselves* the objects of my concern: they are a way into something else: they function as examples of, and analogies to, our senses *as such* and their limitations *as such*, and are used to make points of general application.

My correspondence with Martin led me to read quite widely in some of the literature on sight and blindness. Among other things, this gave me a new understanding of the fact that seeing is something that needs to be *learnt*. It is not at all the case that if an adult who has been blind from childhood recovers his sight he immediately sees what the sighted see. Perhaps this is best understood by considering how the rest of us do, as a matter of fact, learn to see.

Only over a long period do babies learn to pick out particulars in the lighted blur in front of their eyes. It is a process that goes through various stages. At first, light itself is what attracts them. Then they become aware of movement. Then colours. It is a long time before they begin to distinguish shapes –

presumably everything is blurry up till then. A longer period still elapses before they begin to distinguish objects. Only then, apparently, do they acquire a sense of visual space. With that they discover that there are differences of distance, to which they have to adapt themselves. Only through repeated experience can what is seen and what is touched be identified as the same object. Only through experience can sounds be associated with objects that are seen. A baby brings to the learning of all this an intense and rapt concentration for hours of every day over a period of months that spills into years. The whole thing is an unhurried learning process of almost unimaginable complexity and sophistication. And only slowly, very slowly, over this long period of time, does the baby succeed in piecing together the highly variegated and detailed visual world which it will inhabit for the rest of its life. The process absorbs huge amounts of its energy, and much if not most of its interest – and occupies a greater area of the cerebral cortex of its developing brain than any other single activity.

An important point for later consideration is that the baby is not confined to being a passive spectator of this world that it so slowly and painstakingly learns to construct. It is an active participant; and the degree of its participation is something that likewise develops with experience. In all sorts of ways it responds physically to what it sees, relates what it sees to itself, and becomes increasingly an agent in its perceived world – so that in more and more respects its behaviour patterns, and thus also its sense of itself, are interrelated with its experience, and with its responses to the experience, of visually perceived objects. In this way visual experience – fundamental to the particular realization it actually acquires of the existence of other people, and of their distinct identities – gets woven also into the warp and woof of its awareness of the sort of creature that it itself is, and of its place in the world, and thus of its sense of its own identity.

It is out of these considerations that three crucial points arise for someone who is born blind and then acquires sight later in life.

First, he remains incapable of seeing what the rest of us see until after he has gone through a long and elaborate learning process that is almost overwhelming in its demands if these are first encountered in adult life (literally overwhelming for many, as we shall see). For a long time an enormous amount of what comes to him through his eyes is simply unidentified or un-understood, and thus meaningless or disturbing; and he has no idea how he stands in relation to much of it.

Second, because a blind person grows to adulthood learning to do literally everything he can do without the use of his eyes, all of his thoroughly accustomed ways of doing things possess that character, including all the things that he no longer needs to think about, the things that come 'naturally', as we say. All this is part and parcel of the only life he knows, and therefore of his conception of reality, and of how he relates to it – and therefore of his sense of himself, and his own identity. So it is not at all the case that if he acquires sight a lot of things that were difficult before suddenly become easy. The easy, the natural, what feels to him 'him', goes on being what it has always been, especially in view of the fact that his newly acquired sense of sight is so fraught with confusion. The neurologist Oliver Sacks has recorded the approach of such a person to some of the most everyday activities:

He started eating, I observed, in the normal sighted fashion, accurately spearing segments of tomato in his salad. Then, as he continued, his aim grew worse: his fork started to miss its targets, and to hover, uncertainly, in the air. Finally, unable to 'see', or make sense of, what was on his plate, he gave up the effort and started to use his hands, to eat as he used to, as a blind person eats . . . There had been similar reversions, for example, with his shaving, where he would start with a mirror, shaving by sight, with tense concentration. Then the stroke of the razor would become slower, and he would start to peer uncertainly at his face in the mirror, or try to confirm what he saw by touch. Finally, he would turn away from the mirror, or close his eyes, or turn the light off, and finish the job by feel.[1]

Third, a person who has grown up blind has developed a different sort of identity from a sighted person, not just in social and psycho-analytic senses of the term 'identity' but in mechanical and neurological senses too. His brain and nervous system have become physically different.

Conflict and crisis are inevitable if the perceptual habits and strategies of a lifetime are to be changed. Such conflicts are built into the nature of the nervous system itself, for the early-blinded adult who has spent a lifetime adapting and specializing his brain must now ask his brain to reverse all this . . . In the newly sighted, learning to see demands a radical change in neurological functioning and, with it, a radical change in psychological functioning, in self, in identity. The change may be experienced in literally life-and-death terms.[2]

When these three things are realized it will be readily understood that – contrary to what seems to be commonly supposed – for an adult who has been blind since childhood to recover his sight is a traumatic experience. Many of those to

[1] Oliver Sacks, 'To See And Not See', *The New Yorker*, (10 May 1993).
[2] Ibid.

whom it happens do not, alas, cope with it successfully. After an initial period of excitement and hope they start to lose their bearings and become bewildered, then depressed. There are even some who commit suicide. A lot go back to living as if they were blind, even though they no longer are, because that is the only way they feel at home in the world and able to cope with it. Only a minority of their personal histories have a happy ending, and even those reach it only after prolonged and painful difficulties.

Marius von Senden, reviewing every published case over a three-hundred-year period in his classic book 'Space and Sight' (1932), concluded that every newly sighted adult sooner or later comes to a 'motivation crisis' – and that not every patient gets through it. He tells of one patient who felt so threatened by sight (which would have meant his leaving the Asylum for the Blind, and his fiancée there) that he threatened to tear his eyes out; he cites case after case of patients who 'behave blind' or 'refuse to see' after an operation, and of others who, fearful of what sight may entail, refuse operation (one such account, entitled 'L'Aveugle Qui Refuse de Voir', was published as early as 1771). Both Gregory and Valvo dilate on the emotional dangers of forcing a new sense on a blind man – how, after an initial exhilaration, a devastating (and even lethal) depression could ensue.[3]

All this, I believe, throws great light on some of the attitudes displayed by Martin in our correspondence. It also does a great deal to render more credible, and more comprehensible, his claim that quite a number of blind people would not be enthusiastic about seeing again even if it became a possibility for them. I found this statement almost impossible to accept when

[3] Ibid.

he first made it, but now I understand the full force of it. This brings home yet again, as so much that Martin said to me did, how often and how radically the sighted fail to understand the true situation of the blind. (The most elementary misconception of all – that the blind live in darkness – seems to me to be almost universal. What then do they actually live 'in'? The most plausible description I have heard so far from a person with special knowledge is that it is like my apprehension of the space behind the back of my head.) However, the most important thing it brings home – and what I value it for above all else – is what it would be like for us if we were suddenly to acquire an additional sense that was on a par in importance with seeing. The experience would be disorienting, terrifying, traumatic. We would, all of us, have the greatest difficulty in coping with it, and many of us would fail in the attempt. Even the most successful of us would find it frightening. So, far from welcoming a whole new dimension of awareness into the thrilling embrace of our relationship with the world, we should more likely try to reject it, at least in part, and go back (at least in part) to the relationship we had with the world before acquiring the new sense. As T. S. Eliot has famously remarked, human kind cannot bear very much reality. There have been religious writers who have speculated that when the human soul comes face to face with God it cannot bear it and begs to be taken away from the burning, blinding, intolerable presence. Perhaps 'God' here is simply a name for more reality than we can bear.

Altogether, then, my correspondence with Martin launched a dramatic learning process for me. And the aspect of it I valued most was the possibility of insight it offered into the relationship between human beings and those aspects of total reality that are not accessible to their powers of sensory apprehension. I find myself now with a much deeper understanding of

Schopenhauer's remark that if a creature from outside the realm of human limitation were patiently to explain to us what the character is of that part of reality that lies beyond the range of our intellectual and sensory faculties we would not be able to understand what he was talking about. I have to add, though, that Martin has also given me a new understanding of the extent to which this statement needs to be qualified. It is not the case, as Schopenhauer believed, that we would understand nothing at all. We might, with luck, achieve a small but nevertheless worthwhile measure of partial understanding. Even so, most of what there was to understand would be sealed off from all possibility of explanation to us. This would be true not only of attempts to explain the whole of unapprehended reality but of attempts to explain any part of it: getting us to understand the difference that just one single additional sense would make, if the difference were comparable in magnitude to that between seeing and never having seen, would fail. And of course there could easily be many such senses.

The blind/sighted distinction, because it falls inside the area covered by human experience, gives us an opportunity to gain insight into what lies on both sides of the limits that not having one of the senses we do have would have imposed on our conception of the world; and this in turn enables us to form some notion of the sort of limits imposed on us by the possession of human faculties as such, even though in the latter case we are unable to think on both sides of the limits. In other words, because there is already, within our experience, a dividing line that must, or so it seems to me, be analogous in some ways to the dividing line between human experience as such and what lies beyond it, we are able to get an idea of what sort of difference this difference is, despite the fact that we are still not able to form any determinate conception of what it is

215

that lies beyond the limits of possible experience for us. And that being so, just as Martin was able to infer, from the experience he did have, a great deal more than I would have dreamt possible about the nature of the sense he lacked, and what reality is like for those who do not lack it, I find myself wondering whether it might be possible for the rest of us to achieve something corresponding to this with regard to the limitations of our experience as a whole.

When, as my correspondence with Martin proceeded, I tried to discuss these thoughts with other people, I encountered the assumption that I was trying to insinuate unacknowledged religious implications, or even toying with self-indulgent ideas about the supernatural. I am not doing either of these things. The mistaken assumption that I am springs from the apparent inability of some people to shake off their identification of reality, of what there is – the world, Nature – with what human beings experience or can experience. To assume that the two are the same is to make an assumption for which there could never be adequate grounds. It is true that it is an assumption that cannot be disproved, but of course it cannot be proved either, and for reasons I gave earlier it is unlikely in the extreme. As Hume showed, many basic propositions about the world whose truth nearly all of us accept cannot be proved: familiar examples are the existence of an external world, the operation within it of causal relationships, and even that the sun will rise tomorrow. Most statements about the future are of this kind, for it cannot be proved that there will be a future, though of course we feel as certain as we are of anything that there will be. In the same way, for each of us it is logically possible that solipsism is true, yet I believe we are justified in our feeling of certainty that it is not. This is the kind of statement we are making when we say that there are aspects of reality which humans cannot apprehend with the contingent and limited faculties they happen to have: it is not provable, yet, given the circumstances, I do not see how it can fail to be true. This being so, far from talking about something other-worldly when I say this I am talking about the reality we already inhabit – *this* world, apprehended in ways of which we cannot conceive, precisely comparable, for instance, to the way it would look to a sighted non-human if the human race had never had eyes.

There is a serious sense in which there cannot be anything super-real. That which exists unapprehended by us is as real as what we apprehend, in the same way as the visual world is none the less real, and real in a perfectly everyday sense, for the fact that the blind do not experience it. If we were all without sight it would be a transcendental reality for all of us, but that would not transform it into a religious phenomenon. There would be nothing supernatural about it, nothing spiritual or other-worldly, still less anything occult. It would be 'there' in exactly the same way as it is 'there' now, only human beings would not apprehend it. In the same way all those aspects of reality that we do not apprehend must be just as genuinely a part of it, just as hum-drum if you like, just as 'ordinary', as those we do – or just as miraculous, of course: one could put it either way round with equal point. In the sense in which the world of sight is miraculous, the world as it might be apprehended in other ways is also miraculous, but only in that sense. To the extent that, in practice, sighted people take the visual world for granted, so creatures who apprehended it in other ways would, I presume, take that for granted too. The notion that there must be something quasi-magical about whatever might exist beyond the limits of possible human experience is misplaced, and so we stand in need of some sort of demystification of the unknown. All there can possibly be is more of reality, and that is all. If there is a God then he is part, or all, of reality; and if he is permanent then his very permanence makes him, in the most literal meaning of the word, everyday.

An unrelated approach to a not unrelated kind of insight can proceed from the fact that human explanations of natural phenomena have continuing histories. Primitive man starts out by explaining the world to himself in terms of spirits and magic, but in the course of time most such explanations are replaced by other and sometimes better ones. But these in their turn are eventually replaced too. The process is one that never stops. To this day, explanatory theories are constantly being replaced by other theories which are often better, and this is going on all around us not just in the physical sciences but in medicine, sociology, history, economics and all other serious disciplines. And it is simply not possible for people living in a historical period prior to the breakthrough to the scientific understanding of some particular phenomenon to possess an explanation of it that is both rational and accurate. Let us take, for example, electricity. Scientific understanding of electricity is only some 200 years old. Before that time it was impossible for even the very greatest geniuses to understand it, short of making the necessary scientific discoveries themselves, since the required concepts did not as yet exist. Any attempt on their part to provide an explanation in terms of their existing conceptions could only be wrong. Perhaps not surprisingly, when electricity was inexplicable in terms of existing concepts, it was often given a supernatural or occult explanation. This tends to happen with phenomena in general. If people cannot fit something into the framework of their present understanding they are likely to attribute it to supernatural causes, when all the time there may be a non-supernatural explanation that they are unable to conceptualize because the formulation of it lies outside their limitations in time.

This is true not only of theoretical explanations but also of physical devices. Today we think of the heart as a pump, and we are right to do so because its function is to pump the blood round the body. But no one could possibly have thought of the heart as a pump before there were such things as pumps. The concept did not exist, and no one, no matter how perceptive, could have formulated the thought in his mind – unless he were himself to invent the concept, in which case he would be not only the theoretical inventor of the pump but also the discoverer of the circulation of the blood. Now although it is self-evidently true, it is hard for us to take on board the fact that we ourselves, all of us, at all times, are in this position with regard to the entire future growth of all knowledge insofar as it is not now predicted – all not-yet-foreseen discoveries and all not-yet-foreseen inventions. A couple of hundred years from now every well-stocked mind will teem with knowledge and understanding that are totally beyond the bounds of thought for anyone now, as unconceptualizable as quantum physics and relativity theory were to anyone before the eighteenth century, and as un-understandable as were then automotive vehicles, telephones, radios and television sets – objects with which even unintelligent people today are thoroughly at home, and which they find no difficulty in operating.

Here then is another whole world of examples – unlimited in extent – of what are in practice unthinkable thoughts, unconceptualizable concepts and ungraspable realities, based this time not on the fact that the physical sensory and mental faculties of human beings are contingent and limited but on the quite different facts that humans are largely ignorant of what lies ahead of them in time and that their knowledge and understanding of the world tend to grow, often very rapidly, over time. There is nothing transcendental or supernatural or religious about the knowledge and understanding that are by a long way future in time to any given individual, and for that reason unconceptualizable by him. They will arrive in due course with rational explanations attaching to them. But for us to know them *now* would be magic – supernatural in the literal sense of the word. Indeed, knowledge of the future has always been the most wished-for form of the supernatural among human beings. In very ancient times prophets, oracles, augurers and soothsayers were held in the highest awe. In our own more frivolous age the most popular form of the occult is having one's fortune foretold, whether from stars, tealeaves, playing cards, crystal balls, hands or dreams. But it is only *knowledge* of the future that is, or would be if we had it, supernatural. The future itself is not supernatural: it is merely history that we have not yet come to. A time will arrive when any given part of what is now future will be past, and then it will be all one with history as a whole, specifically as well known as – and in fact, because of modern information technology, almost certainly better known than – those parts of history that we know today in greatest detail. There is nothing in the least bit magic about the future, yet we can easily slide into supposing that there is, because *knowledge* of it would be magic, and because we wish for that knowledge so thirstily.

In a similar way, knowledge of the present through a sense that we do not possess would be magical, not because there would have been anything in the least magical about our having been endowed with six senses instead of five, but because we do not have that particular sense. In both cases the fact that we lack the input that we do lack is contingent, happenstance; and yet it does mean that only by transcending the natural order could we acquire it. For us now to have knowledge of the future would be supernatural, but when the future becomes present and we acquire knowledge of it in the normal way there will be nothing supernatural about it at all, neither about what happens nor about our knowledge of it. We shall then be in possession of entirely natural explanations. It is simply that they are not available to us now. And in this case no number of additional senses would make them available. Our ignorance is due not to the fact that we lack enough sensory input in the present, but to the fact that we lack the necessary concepts. This has nothing to do with how intelligent we are: the stupidest people will one day, and quite soon, be thoroughly conversant with ideas, processes and devices that are unimaginable to even geniuses in the present.

A curious aspect of all this is that although everyone knows that what I am saying must be true we find it surprisingly difficult *in practice* to think and behave in the light of it. We almost cannot help trying to construct a coherent view of the world out of the input available to us at this moment, and then proceeding as if reality itself corresponded to that. Although it defies all the considerations I have been bringing forward, we do it just the same. Practical considerations have great influence on us in this respect. We feel we have no alternative but to get on with our lives; we cannot live without taking action; and we cannot act without making decisions and choices: it is impossible for us to take into account considerations that we cannot even conceptualize: so the best we can do is make the most we can of the materials we have. This means we have no better option than to live *as if* the utmost that we can apprehend at this moment is the way things are. As a basis for practical living I can have little to quarrel with in that. I start to object seriously only when people really do believe – and it is clear that there are many who do believe – that the limits of what we can apprehend are the limits of what there is. I assert that, if only we stop to think, we *know* that this is not the case, and is indeed on a very massive scale not the case: we know that the entire corpus of human knowledge and understanding available to those of us living at around the year 2000 is going to appear small in the eyes of any observers that there may be living around the year 3000, probably a great deal more tiny and impoverished than the mental world of 1066 appears to us now. We know all this. How, then, can we perpetrate the almost unbelievably crude error of identifying the limits of reality with the limits of what happens to be intelligible to us now?

The huge and all-pervading metaphysical mistake that we tend to make because of the limitations that our position in time places on what we can apprehend has important features in common with the one we make about the limits that the nature of our sensory and mental apparatus places on what we can apprehend – though of course the two mistakes are by no means the same in all respects. In both cases, though, limits that we are unable to transcend are imposed on what we can conceptualize. In both cases these limits are limitations on us, on our powers of apprehension, not limitations inherent in the nature of whatever it is that exists independently of our experience. In both cases this and other considerations give us grounds for near-certainty that there is more to reality than we are in a position to apprehend. Yet in both cases we ignore this fact for most if not all of the time and base our view of total reality on an unspoken but tenaciously held assumption that the limits of what exists correspond to the limits of what we can make sense of. Finally, in both cases there is something paradoxical about the very making of the mistake: on the one hand it is so easy to see why we make it that doing so seems almost inevitable; but on the other hand, precisely because it is obvious that the error is there lying in wait for us to fall into, one would expect it to be a notorious and obvious nonsense that everyone knew about, and no reflective person would perpetrate.

Let me put the case about the limits of our sensory equipment differently, as a succession of five points. First, we know that our sensory and mental apparatus is contingent. Second, we know that reality is itself contingent. Third, we know that other creatures possess senses that we do not have, and that through these senses they apprehend reality in ways that we do not. Fourth, we know it is possible that we might have had senses additional to those we do have, senses that would have made as much difference to our apprehension of the world as the difference between seeing and not seeing; and not only one such sense but an indefinite number of them, as different from one another as sight, hearing and touch. Fifth, we know from our observation of the born-blind that it comes naturally to them to form a conception of the world that is coherent and yet contains no direct visual experience. Putting these five points together one might suppose that we sighted people would draw the obvious conclusion that although it comes to us naturally to form a coherent view of the world out of the resources available to us, the view of the world that we thus form presumably leaves out more than it includes, and we are unable to conceptualize what it is that it leaves out.

As a university student I was taught that in philosophy the term 'the world' is a technical term meaning either the totality of what exists or the totality of actual and possible human experience, and that the two concepts were equivalent. The mistaken belief that they are equivalent is built not only into philosophy in the empirical tradition but into much other philosophy as well. To take a well-known book as an example, it is foundational to Wittgenstein's *Tractatus*. The main text of that work begins with the words: 'The world is everything that is the case. The world is the totality of facts ... The world is determined by the facts, and by these being *all* the facts.' But before long Wittgenstein is saying (3.01): 'The totality of true thoughts is a picture of the world.' The correspondence between the actually existing and the thinkable could scarcely be more boldly, and of course mistakenly, asserted.

An important part of the barrier that gets between us and a fuller understanding is psychological. When I try to put considerations of the kind I have been discussing before professional philosophers they do not normally leap at them and get excited by their implications. Rather, they tend to take on a resigned and distracted air, agree that these things are indeed true, and then almost immediately change the subject and revert to their accustomed frame of reference. If brought back to the point, they tend to protest that the truths in question are such as not to be usable in thought. Since not-yet-existing concepts are not available to us we cannot think with them. So if we are to think at all we have to, and can only, do our thinking without them. Likewise, if it is true that we are imprisoned for life in an epistemological cage, permanently unable to look at whatever lies outside it except through its bars – in other words, if we are for ever unable to conceive of non-epistemological reality in other than epistemological terms which are not only sense-dependent but contingent upon the nature of the particular senses we happen to possess – then that is a fact, and has to be accepted and lived with, because nothing we can ever do will transcend it. What would be wrong, such people contend, would be to acknowledge the truth of this and then persist in trying to transcend it – trying to think the unthinkable, know the unknowable, express the inexpressible. There are only too many thinkers who have tried to do this, but the result is always (our interlocutors would say) splurge. Some such thinkers have been honest and self-deluded, others have been charlatans, but both kinds have succeeded only in producing verbiage without significant content, empty utterance, exhaust.

My point, however, is not that we should indulge ourselves in splurge. I agree entirely that the unknowable will remain unknown, the inexpressible unexpressed. We shall go to our graves not knowing what the truth is about the things that matter to us most. Existentially, this is the hardest thing in life to bear. I am not suggesting that we ignore these facts. On the contrary, I am suggesting that we face up to them properly, perhaps for the first time. What I want to insist on is that the limitations placed on human understanding by the nature of our equipment and, separately, by our location in time, have all-important implications for what we can know and for what we can understand, and therefore that a recognition of these limitations and their implications should be allowed to have its profound natural effect on our thinking. The consequences of such a change would be so far-reaching that no one person could possibly predict them all. There are, however, four whose importance I would wish to urge immediately.

The first is that the difference I am talking about is so great that once it had established itself it would be impossible for people fully to understand how human beings could ever have thought as we do, so flatly contradictory is this to so many obvious facts. The notion that reality is co-extensive with what we can understand, or what we can think, will one day be, I am sure, of self-evident falsity. This in turn will put a permanent end to attempts to formulate systematic holistic explanations of a lasting character – we shall have realized that any such explanation would have to be wrong for each of two separate sets of reasons, one to do with our physical equipment and its limitations, the other to do with our location in time and *its* limitations. As regards this realization a threefold qualification is in order. First, 'wrong' in this context includes among its possible meanings 'radically inadequate', something that may perhaps be all right as far as it goes but does not go far enough. Second, the longing for an understanding of the whole could still function fruitfully as one of the driving forces behind investigation even though it is a longing for the unattainable. And thus, third, 'understanding of the whole' can function effectively as an ideal, a regulative idea, so long as it is understood that, being such, it is absolutely unattainable, something which to all eternity is to be approached only asymptotically, at least by human beings. However, even when these three qualifications have been allowed their full weight, human knowledge and understanding can still only be seen as not just little and limited but, above all else, scrappy – a few arbitrarily related, if related at all, bits and pieces. We are forever groping around in the dark and bumping into things, knowing little, understanding almost nothing. And that will be the human condition for as long as humans are human.

My second prediction is that this new perspective is likely to bring with it a certain humility. The very greatest thinkers of all, from Socrates to Einstein, have always realized that they knew next to nothing, and have possessed a rare and insightful understanding of at least some of the reasons why this is so. Lesser thinkers, however, have not usually resembled them in this respect. Indeed, it has even been a generally misunderstood characteristic of the great, attributed to a certain saintliness of character on their part rather than appreciated as one of their intellectual achievements. Humility in turn ought to beget tolerance, not of low standards but of the different and the new – 'openness' perhaps would be a better word than 'tolerance', because serious thinkers are bound to be intolerant of a great deal of the thinking that passes ordinary muster. 'I may be wrong, but if I am it can't be for *that* reason' is bound to remain their attitude to a good deal of the comment they encounter.

My third prediction is that it is not true to say that thinking that takes full cognizance of our human limitations will be inhibited from making worthwhile advances. On the contrary, the book most widely regarded among serious students of philosophy as the greatest philosophical work to have been produced since the ancient Greeks, Kant's *Critique of Pure Reason*, is devoted largely to an analysis of the nature of some of these limitations, and succeeded in making the biggest single forward step in philosophy for more than 2000 years. Nor can it be claimed that, after Kant, further progress can be made on a big scale only if one writes *about* our limitations, as against accepting the reality of them in thinking about other things. Schopenhauer believed firmly that Kant had got hold of the right end of the stick, and incorporated the better part of his epistemological analysis into his own, and then went on to make some of the most significant advances that anyone has made since Kant. It happens to be my view – though there is no need for my readers to share it if I am to make my point – that most of the best philosophy since Kant has been in some important sense Kantian. Nietzsche proclaimed that it was the reading of Schopenhauer that turned him into a philosopher. Wittgenstein's *Tractatus* is a thoroughgoingly Schopenhauerian work. And Popper always regarded himself, rightly in my opinion, as a reconstructed Kantian. At the heart of the work of all these thinkers, especially that of Schopenhauer, Wittgenstein and Popper, is a Kantian concern for the limits of what can be known, or expressed, or understood. And the magnitude of their achievement demolishes the idea that to acknowledge insuperable limitations is to be unduly limited. The notion that acknowledgement of such limits diminishes creativity is on all fours with the idea that there is now no further room left for the writing of original tunes among the permutations and combinations of notes that are possible in traditional keys – an idea that has frequently been expressed since Schubert, and refuted by every good composer there has been during that time. It recalls the advice given to the young Max Planck by his professor not to waste his career by going in for research in physics, because more or less everything there was to find out in physics had already been found out. The boot, in each case, is on the other foot. It might be going too far to say that only if a composer writes in traditional keys does he stand any chance of writing good tunes, but there are still a lot more of that sort than of any other sort. The situation in philosophy is parallel: it would be going too far to say that only if one takes Kant on board can one make significant advances – the Logical Positivists were essentially a pre-Kantian throw-back, a regression to Hume, yet they have some worthwhile achievements to their credit – but I do not see how there can be any really fundamental advance in philosophy that does not move forward from Kant's discoveries. The all-important fact he established of there being untranscendable limits to what is intelligible to us does nothing to block off any path that ever actually existed, or ever could have existed. On the contrary, it defines the main challenge that confronts us. This challenge is not to transcend untranscendable limits but to conduct our serious thinking in the light of a recognition of their existence, and to deepen our penetration into the implications of the fact that they exist, and of what we can understand their nature to be. There is, I am certain, a very great deal more to find out than we have yet found out; and there will be great philosophers in the future, just as there have been in the past.

My fourth prediction is that if we really do absorb into ourselves the realization that little can be known, it will affect our estimate of the place of intellect in human life. For if our intellects can give us, at best, only a little knowledge, and that scrappy, it is natural that we should try to supplement this with other ways of coming to terms with experience and trying to understand reality. My mind turns first of all to the arts. These can nourish us with all kinds of insights – new ways of looking at things, new ways of understanding things – which may be metabolized into our being, and yet do not constitute knowledge in the sense of anything that is empirically testable. They may be of immense value to us, and greatly enrich our lives, but they do not constitute rational knowledge in the normal sense, and we should never slide into the error of supposing that they do. I have met many religious people who fall into errors of a related kind: they tell me they *know* that God exists, and they *know* we have souls that survive the deaths of our bodies. But the fact is that they do not know these things in any sense of the word 'know' that can be respected. At best they know them in something like the way I know that Beethoven's symphonies are better than Bruckner's. My conviction to this effect may feel unshakable, but if someone who loved the music of both and knew it well argued intelligently to the contrary, there would be no inter-subjectively valid way in which I could refute him. No matter how long we argued, we should almost certainly end up with each still clinging to his own conviction. Convictions of this kind are not knowledge, and we should never lose sight of that fact, no matter how strong the subjective feelings of certainty are that seize us in their grip. The difference can be a matter of life or death: quite a lot of human beings have been prepared to die for their convictions, but nobody dies for knowledge.

How we know whatever it is we do know is a profoundly mysterious matter. Many suppose that for something to be knowledge it has to be capable of rational demonstration, but on analysis that view turns out to be untenable. One reason why it is not tenable hangs on the nature of argument. In any piece of deductive logic each step of the argument is necessarily entailed by what has gone before; but that must mean that the argument

229

itself does not contribute anything new to the content of our conclusion, which has been carried forward *in full* through each intervening step. A valid argument demonstrates that its conclusions follow from its premises, but it does nothing to establish the truth of either. If one and only one person is President of the United States in 1994, and the President of the United States in 1994 is Chinese, and Bill Clinton is President of the United States in 1994, then Bill Clinton is Chinese. That is an immaculately true statement and a 100 per cent valid argument. But it does not prove that Bill Clinton is Chinese. Bill Clinton is not Chinese, and no valid argument will prove that he is. In any valid argument the truth of a conclusion is guaranteed only if all the premises are true. But that means that our knowledge of the truth of the premises cannot be established by the argument itself, for in that case the argument would be circular. Only independently of the conclusions of an argument can its premises be known to be true. And if those premises themselves are entailed by impeccably conducted arguments this means they are the conclusions of other arguments with other premises – which in their turn call for validation from outside the arguments of which they are premises. So in the end all the knowledge we have, if we have any at all, must go back to, and rest on, something that is not argument, not deductive logic, not a rational demonstration that such-and-such premises entail such-and-such conclusions. Anything we can know at all must be known independently of rational argument in the sense of logical demonstration. That being so, the widely held view that only what can be demonstrated by rational argument can be known for certain could hardly be more wrong: the truth is that nothing that we know about the world can be established as knowledge by rational argument alone.

Obviously these are deep waters. What can the kind of knowledge we think of as rational be supported by if not by rational argument? It would be easy at this point for me to be misunderstood as saying that rational argument has no part in knowledge, and this is not what I am saying, nor is it what I believe. Rational argument does indeed have a role to play in knowledge: but it is not the role that we have been considering up to now. Knowledge can never be *derived* from argument: the propositions and hypotheses that we put forward as constituting what we 'know' are not arrived at as the conclusions of rational arguments, nor can they be so arrived at, for the reasons given. However, if those propositions are to have a serious claim to constitute knowledge they must be able to withstand criticism and tests, and it is with these processes that rational argument comes into the picture: the critical discussion of theories involves rational argument; and so, if only implicitly, do tests. But we need to be in possession of our theory before we can critically discuss it or test it: so rational argument is not part of the way in which we *arrive* at our claims to knowledge, it is part of the way we test them after they have been made, and thus a part of what establishes their title to knowledge. Where, then, do the hypotheses that we test come from? The answer is, it does not matter where they come from. They may be purest invention; or they may derive from direct observation, or past experience, or calculation, or the revision of past expectations or theories; we may have got them from a colleague, or a teacher, or a friend, from reading or from hearsay; they may be no more than part of the conventional wisdom. Since their source is not what confers truth on them it does not matter what the source is. Some of the most valuable advances in human knowledge that have ever been made, in the sciences as well as elsewhere, have been, literally, dreamt; and more than that have resulted from mistakes. An incalculable number started out as hunches that were followed up and happened to pay off. If I were a scientist and published a new theory it would not occur to anyone to check it by making enquiries about me or my qualifications, nor to get in touch with me and ask me by what processes of thought I had arrived at my ideas. The reason why it would not occur to anyone to do this is that, if they did, it would tell them nothing about the validity of the ideas, and would be irrelevant to the question of their truth. Their truth is to be supported, or disconfirmed, only by critical evaluation of the theory itself – by scrutiny, measurement, calculation, discussion, observation, testing, experiment, and so on, the nature of all these in this particular case being dictated by the theory itself, and being the same regardless of the processes by which the theory was arrived at. If the scientific world came to regard it as a contribution to knowledge they would do so not because of anything to do with the way it had been arrrived at but because of its success in resisting the most rigorous criticism and testing.

This fact, that valid ideas can come from anywhere, is of the highest importance in our imaginative and creative lives – and therefore of the highest human importance. Properly understood, it should make us intellectually open, curious, adventurous. If none of our knowledge owes its status as knowledge to the fact that it has been arrived at by rational argument then it is no criticism of something's claim to be knowledge that it has not been arrived at by rational argument. Knowledge *in any case* has to be something different from that. The mistaken view retained by so many intellectuals and academics of the role of rationality in intellectual life makes them pusillanimous: often they are afraid of saying anything that they cannot demonstrate by argument – and of course in the nature of things that is not much. If we believed only what we could prove we would believe almost nothing, and would be sceptics – and then we would find it impossible to live, because to live is to choose, and choice inescapably involves beliefs and expectations. If we are to live at all we have constantly to, in the popular British phrase, 'suck it and see': try something and see how it works, or see how we react to it; dip a toe in the water, probe, test things out; in other words put our hopes or expectations up against experience and see if the two clash. This is what constitutes testing at the common sense level, and we are all doing it much of the time. It is the way we learn most of what we know. We arrive at this knowledge not by argument but by speculating and then testing the speculation, putting more and more weight on the foot that finds a firm hold, withdrawing it the moment we feel a hint of anything giving way beneath it. This is what constitutes true rationality. It involves a willingness to venture, to chance, to have a go – and of course, as an indispensable part of the whole process, to acknowledge at once if a conjecture is mistaken. To go on insisting that it is right after it has begun to clash with reality is the surest way to disaster. In fact, to want to be right all the time is at odds with any true exploration – which is always a matter of testing hypotheses – and therefore with any true life of the mind.

The fact that the chief task of rationality is to test to breaking point whatever hypotheses we are prepared to entertain is the main defence we have against the greatest of all intellectual temptations, namely self-indulgence – the temptation to believe what it comforts us to believe, or what fits our temperament, or suits our convenience. This is the line of least resistance, and many are those who take it: if something could possibly be true, and they would like it to be true, they believe it. No doubt we all fall some of the way into temptation where self-interest is concerned. But every serious thinker regards it as an intellectual evil, not as something to be accepted but as something to be repudiated, fought against, kept as far away from us as possible, its effect on our thinking minimized, because it leads to the replacement of truth by comforting illusions. Anyone who *recommends* beliefs on the grounds of their comfortingness or convenience is an anti-rational person, a renouncer of serious thought and an enemy of the pursuit of truth. Even so, a very large number of people do it, and there are some whole fields of thought, for instance religious thought, in which it is common practice.

One of the chief practical problems facing us in our attempts to achieve real understanding and insight is the problem of how to be open without being self-indulgent – how to remain actively willing to consider new ideas without falling into the trap of believing whatever appeals to us. This calls for perpetual self-awareness and self-criticism – self-criticism above all – and an unsleeping acknowledgement that the real truth-values and probability-values of our beliefs are independent of our wishes. The temptation to believe that something is true because it could be and we would like it to be is a destroyer of honest thinking that never goes out of business. Furthermore, it offers a resting place, whereas true enquiry has no resting place.

Like a lot of the most important truths, these are things one has always known, but apprehends now in a new light. Many will say they are obvious; but they cannot be genuinely obvious to anyone who supposes that there is no reality outside the range of possible human experience, or that there is even a serious chance of reality's being co-equivalent to possible experience; or that there is a possibility of our catching reality as it is in the net of our understanding; or that knowledge we can attain to now will not be superseded in the future. If the folly of these ideas were indeed obvious, many human beings, including many philosophers, would think in quite different ways from the ways they do.

Yours ever,
Bryan Magee

GENERAL INDEX

a priori knowledge 95
abilities, effect of extra sense on 11
abstract concepts 133
academics, and the senses 142
adaptation, human potential for 143
aesthetics, visual 37–8, 109, 135–6
Anglo-Saxon philosophy 24
animals:
   differentiated from humans 149
   knowledge possessed by 31, 94–5,
     158–8, 162
argument, nature of 229–32
Aristotle, on seeing 35, 59–60, 134–5
Armstrong, David 89 164
arts, the:
   as form of communication 152
   insights provided by 229
   knowledge and 155–7
   significance of 154
   visual: typical objections to 135–6
awareness, *see* consciousness
Ayer, A. J. 150

ball games 37, 66, 70–71, 127–8
Basis Problem 150
become-blind, adjustment made by
   188–90
become-blind, *see also* blindness, as
   bereavement; Hull, John
beliefs, as recommended for
   convenience 233–4
Berkeley, Bishop George xii, 139
blind:
   communication with others 181–2
   community formed with sighted 92

credence given by, to claims of
   sighted 10, 88
as denied access to some areas of
   knowledge 47, 125–6
differences in experience between
   sighted and 68–9
and equality 116
from birth, *see* blind-from-birth
hypothetical world where all are
   51–3, 146
perception of surroundings 71–5,
   125–7, 191
policies to isolate/integrate 61–2
positive spirit evident among 51,
   57, 68, 186–7, 188
social interaction 63, 74
as underestimating gap between
   themselves and sighted 127–9
world of being as non-existent for
   138
blind, *see also* become-blind; blind-
   from-birth
blind-from-birth:
   ability of, to use and understand
     visual terms 15–16, 27–8, 54, 78–
     9, 102–3, 110–12
   aspects of sight inaccessible to 37–8
   and conceptual meanings 107–8
   deprivations of 48–9, 91–2
   experiential awareness of a lack on
     part of? 19
   and 'knowing a person' 2–3
   and knowledge about sight 88
   opinions on sight from 43, 73–5
   propositional knowledge of,

General Index

sight, *see also* blindness: visual
    experience; visual terms
sighted:
    blind patronized by 67
    conceptions of, as mainly vision-
        derived 136
    differing importance given to sight
        by 58, 142
    as exaggerating importance of
        sight 34, 54–60, 62, 208
    experience of sight the same
        among? 171
    experiential differences between
        blind and 37, 60, 87
    language usefulness
        underestimated by 56–7
    non-visual senses underused by
        56–7, 67
    overestimating gap between
        themselves and blind 127
    personal relations with blind
        64–7
    possibility of blindness for 57
    social contacts less varied than
        those of blind 64–7
solipsism 216
spatial dimension 108, 176, 206
stairs, blind people and 56–7
subconscious mind 143
super-reality 217–18
symbols, types 153–4
'sympathetic' understanding 107,
    110–11
    types 111

tastes:
    describing 29–30, 97–101
    increasing one's knowledge of
        162–3
things, 'separation from world of'
    39–40, 71–2
time:
    the blind and 201–6
    organization of 201–3
    passage of 204–5
touch, sense of 2, 63, 136

understanding:
    barriers to 218–25
    meaning and 102–12
    types 107
unknowable, the, indications of our
    relationship to xiii

Vaihinger, Hans 23, 167–8
VINE (Vision Is Not Essential) 57,
    187, 188
'visionism' 70, 179–83
visual concepts, for blind-from-birth
    33, 37, 103–4, 107, 109, 133
visual experience:
    admitted by blind-from-birth to
        exist 46
    as 'foundational to ordinary living'
        36, 60, 63
    lack of: effect on concept of reality
        208
    phenomenology of, and blind-
        from-birth 31
    as referring to 'out there' rather
        than 'in here' 139, 170–71
    as uniform from person to person 36
visual terms 11–14, 104
    ability of blind-from-birth to use
        and understand 15–16, 27–8, 54,
        78–9, 102–3, 110–12
    bearing non-visual concepts 107
    experiential meaning of 111–12
    people as conceived in 174–5

wave-motions 21–2
Wells, H. G., *The Country of the Blind*
    10, 20, 50
Wittgenstein, Ludwig 23, 26, 96, 97,
    123, 153, 167–8
    followers of 15, 34, 35
    Tractatus 223, 227
words:
    associations and resonances
        106
    power of 112
words, *see also* visual terms
world, defined 223